MW01065101

Random Thoughts From a Simple Believer

Walk with HIM!!

Tammie R Williams

WESTBOW
PRESS®
A DIVISION OF THOMAS NELSON
& ZONDERVAN

WestBow Press books may be ordered through booksellers or by contacting:

WestBow Press
A Division of Thomas Nelson & Zondervan
1663 Liberty Drive
Bloomington, IN 47403
www.westbowpress.com
1 (866) 928-1240

ISBN: 978-1-5127-3518-5 (sc)
ISBN: 978-1-5127-3519-2 (hc)
ISBN: 978-1-5127-3517-8 (e)

Library of Congress Control Number: 2016904601

Print information available on the last page.

WestBow Press rev. date: 03/30/2016

Introduction

I have to start by mentioning what actually started me on this little endeavor of writing down my random thoughts. When I was in college, I took a running class. For four months I was a runner. Later, when I experienced changes in my life (getting married, having children, and pursuing a career), I put the thought in the back of my mind: *I will be a runner again.* The next thing I knew, it was the month of my fiftieth birthday, and I thought, *Wow! I am not a runner.* So I started running. What started out as four and a half minutes of walking interspersed with thirty seconds of jogging—for a total of twenty minutes each time—three times a week became, within nine months, sixty minutes a day of running five to six miles. (I have since toned it down to four miles daily, and I force myself to take at least one day a week off from running. I tend to do things to the extreme, which is a thought to be fleshed out later.) Now, two years after my fiftieth birthday, I am still running, although I must admit that I run on a treadmill. "Real" runners may not put me into their category, but I consider myself a runner.

While running on the treadmill, I watch Epworth Methodist Church's ministry program on Channel 6 out of Chickasha, Oklahoma. During this time, I read and study the Bible verses provided. There is a continuous scrolling of verses from Genesis to Revelation in random order, which leads me to have random thoughts about the applications of the Word of God. I decided to write down some of these random thoughts.

I have a passion for the young people and parents of today. We all receive many mixed messages, which begin at an early age, over the course of our lives. How can we not be surprised when people are confused about who they are in Christ? Many do not know who He is, let alone who they are in Him. Maybe by witnessing my thought process and reading the ideas I share, someone can come to know Christ and His power. Also, we, who are further along in our faith may be able to figure out a way to help others know Him, which will lead them to know who they are in Him.

If there was something from your youth that you often said you were going to do or be, you should know that it is never too late. Just get started, and then run with it. "Being confident of this that He who began a good work in you, will carry it on to completion until the day of Christ Jesus" Philippians 1:6 (NIV).

My First Attempt to Get Started on This Book (written Fall 2010)

I am currently at a personal crossroads. I have been teaching in a public school system for the past twenty-eight years. I've spent the last twenty-two years teaching at the same high school. I am literally beginning to see some children of my previous students graduate. In February 2010, I reached the magical age of eighty in teaching, which means that my age (fifty-two years) plus my experience (twenty-eight years) equal eighty, so I was officially eligible for retirement benefits from the great state of Oklahoma. Since I had no clue what I wanted to do when I graduated from high school, again, I thought I would stay on for another year. I took the approach that I would be a fifth-year senior until I figured out what to do with the rest of my adult life. (I hope you understand that I actually did graduate from high school, in 1976. I just consider myself to be a person who has been a forever high school student, since I taught in the same high school for the past twenty-two years.) Now that I have begun to teach the 2010–2011 school year, I am wondering, *What was I thinking?* I think I should have graduated with the class of 2010.

When others come to me for advice, my first response is usually, "Have you written your thoughts down?" When they answer no, I add, "Well, maybe you should. When you later read what you wrote, you might better understand what you are struggling with. If not, bring what you wrote to me. Maybe I can help you read between the lines. It is amazing how much clearer your thoughts become when you write them down and then read them." So I guess I am taking my own advice. I have no clue what to do next, so I am just writing down what I think. Maybe I will figure something out for myself, or—even better—maybe my thoughts will help someone else figure something out.

Finally. . . .

The fall 2012, one lovely morning, I sent to a good number of my friends a text that my thoughts became something more than my thoughts in my head. The next thing I knew, I was regularly sending text messages to people. Most of the recipients seemed to enjoy the text messages. Many responded to me, saying that a particular message encouraged them or made them think. I found the experience to be most fun when someone would respond and say that what I had written was exactly what he or she needed to hear that day. Some people asked me to stop sending the text messages after they had received a couple. (I was glad they were honest with me. Asking me to stop sending the messages was better than continuing to receive them and rolling their eyes, wishing I would just stop.) After a while, I began to post my thoughts to my Facebook page, which I continue to do. Now three years later I have been prodded to put my posts together in a book. And so it began with this text:

If you missed the sunrise this morning because you were sleeping or because there was cloud cover in your area, don't worry, as God has provided you with a never-ending Son who rose and who promised never to leave you or forsake you! Walk with Him today! Be blessed!

There are different kinds of spiritual gifts but they all come from the same spirit. There are different ways to serve but we all serve the same Lord. And there are different ways God works in people, but it is the same God who works in all of us to do everything.

—1 Corinthians 12:4–6 (ERV)

This verse jumped out at me one morning. Actually I had been looking for something completely different in Scripture, but these words caught my heart. Maybe it was because I had become very frustrated with the bandwagon type of thinking being pushed by the world. If you aren't on the bandwagon of the day, then you are amiss or are not a caring person. If you have an opinion that is different from the overriding opinion of the day, then once again there is something wrong with you. Sometimes it seems the world is pushing a one-size-fits-all kind of life for people.

I know that the Bible verse provided above doesn't seem to match what is being said here, but hold on. The verse is talking about the creativity of God and how He gives different gifts. It also indicates that there are different ways to serve and that God works differently in the lives of His believers. Right? But how many times do we as believers think there is a one-size-fits-all pattern in our relationship with Christ? Some people think that all relationships with Christ should look the same. If they don't look as some people want them to look, then the conclusion is that somebody or something must be wrong. This implies that some people are only looking at the gifts, the service, and the work done in others' lives—but that is not where we should be looking. The key is where these gifts, service, and work come from. The gifts come from God, and they are never greater than the One who gives them. The service is for God, and it is never greater than the One being served. Similarly, the work (change) in each person's life is never greater than the One who did the work.

If we take our focus off the parts of life that point to us and then place our focus on the One on whom should be focused, then the differences that seem to cause chaos and discord between us might go away. We would be united in our use of the gifts that we have been given from the One our service is for, and we would be celebrating the work He has done in each of our lives instead of comparing it with the work He has done in others' lives.

Walk with Him! Be blessed!

We don't yet see things clearly. We're squinting in a fog, peering through a mist. But it won't be long before the weather clears and the sun shines bright! We'll see it all then, see it all as clearly as God sees us, knowing him directly just as he knows us!

—1 Corinthians 13:12 (MSG)

When I was sitting in the dark without electricity because of a thunderstorm, this verse was the first one I came to. I love how the Lord can take a moment of my life and then connect His Word to that very moment. This Bible quotation reminds me that the Lord only allows us to see in part for now. Someday we will see His fullness. And because of His perfect timing in pointing me to this passage, I am reminded that He sees us fully even in moments that may seem very small to us. Those moments are very important to Him.

Walk with Him! Be blessed!

It is not fancy hair, gold jewelry, or fine clothes that should make you beautiful. No, your beauty should come from inside you—the beauty of a gentle and quiet spirit. That beauty will never disappear. It is worth very much to God.

—1 Peter 3:3–4 (ERV)

There is a saying that goes, "You can put lipstick on a pig, but it is still a pig." The verse above is saying the same thing. No matter how you dress up an unkind, unwise, self-centered person, that person is still unkind, unwise, and self-centered—even if he or she is beautiful on the outside. A quiet, gentle spirit becomes even more beautiful to God over time. Outward beauty can only be maintained for so long. Eventually time has its impact. But inward beauty, that which comes from the Word of God, continues to become more beautiful over time, as it becomes who we are. The Word is the "makeup" that gives us the beauty of Christ. And the beauty of Christ is eternal and never fades. Walk with Him! Be blessed!

Before the world began, the Word was there. The Word was with God, and the Word was God. He was there with God in the beginning. Everything was made through him, and nothing was made without him. In him there was life, and that life was a light for the people of the world.

—John 1:1–4 (ERV)

This will happen when the special child is born. God will give us a son who will be responsible for leading the people. His name will be "Wonderful Counselor, Powerful God, Father Who Lives Forever, Prince of Peace."

—Isaiah 9:6 (ERV)

Today your Savior was born in David's town. He is the Messiah, the Lord.

—Luke 2:11 (ERV)

When he tasted the wine, he said, "It is finished." Then he bowed his head and died.

—John 19:30 (ERV)

Later, Jesus appeared again to his followers by Lake Galilee. This is how it happened.

—John 21:1 (ERV)

After the Lord Jesus said these things to his followers, he was carried up into heaven. There, Jesus sat at the right side of God.

—Mark 16:19 (ERV)

The Lord Himself will come down from heaven with a loud command, with the voice of the archangel, and with the trumpet call of God. And the people who have died and were in Christ will rise first.

—1 Thessalonians 4:16 (ERV)

"Jesus is the reason for the season." "Christmas is over." "Another Christmas has come and gone." All of these are things I have heard and have said around Christmastime. Once it dawned on me that the Christmas story, including the birth of Jesus, which we celebrate in the month of December, doesn't end just because the Christmas decorations come down. We are actually living the Christmas story. It began when God created life. Christ was there; everything was created through Him (John 1:1). The story continues through the prophecy of Christ's birth (Isaiah 9:6) and includes the many other times that His birth is promised in the Old Testament. His birth is proclaimed all throughout the four gospels and elsewhere in the New Testament, especially Luke 2:11. His birth takes us to the cross, where He said, "It is finished." This doesn't mean the story ended. It actually means that the story was to be continued, picked up three days later, when He began appearing to many (John 21:1). After telling the disciples He would send to them the Holy Spirit, they saw Him ascend to heaven, where He told them He was going to be seated at the right hand of God (Mark 16:19), which brings us to where we are now in the story, the point where we are awaiting His promised return (Thessalonians 4:16). Wow, oh wow, the Christmas story is still being written! How amazing is that? And we are characters in the story! From the beginning, when the author (Creator) began writing the Christmas story, He knew we would be written into it. He knew that we would be here at this time, waiting for Christ's return. We may not know what the author will write into this story between now and Christ's return, but we do know that this is how this story is going to end and begin (in eternity). Christ will return and we will be joining Him in glory. Walk with Him! Be blessed!

Immediately, something that looked like fish scales fell off Saul's eyes. He was able to see! Then he got up and was baptized.

—Acts 9:18 (ERV)

Saul, who later took the name Paul, was very passionate about what he believed before he had his encounter with Christ. He truly believed that his persecution of people who followed Christ was the right thing to be doing. He also thought it was necessary to stop the spread of what was coming, which went against what he believed. It was only after he encountered Christ that he realized how wrong his beliefs were.

I love how the Lord made Saul (Paul) literally blind for three days. Unbeknownst to Saul, he had been blind his entire life until he was confronted by Jesus. There are many people in the world today just like Saul who are walking around totally blind and yet have no clue they can't see. They have been deceived into thinking that their vision is 20/20. All the while they can't see the Truth, because the scales of sin have yet to be removed from their eyes. There are many followers of Christ who haven't yet allowed Christ to remove the scales that are blinding them from seeing who they are in Him and, more important, who He truly is. Whatever the reason these people's sight hasn't been restored to perfection through Christ, or do they know their vision can be made crystal clear, but only through encountering Christ like Saul did, by having an encounter with Christ that makes them completely abandon what they once thought was true in order to adopt what Christ says is true.

Walk with Him! Be blessed!

God gave us the ability to think about his world, but we can never completely understand everything he does. And yet, he does everything at just the right time.

—Ecclesiastes 3:11 (ERV)

Our ability to think was given to us by God, but in our human arrogance we see our ability as being greater than the One who gave it to us. We have become so confident in the intelligence we have been given that we have begun to see ourselves (humankind) as the ones who can make things happen just by being smart enough and thinking enough. We can manipulate and control things to the point that we, who were created by God, believe that we no longer need Him and can function and live on our own. Now that is arrogance! Looking at life that way would be like a partially done painting saying to the paintbrush, "I've got this. I can finish this masterpiece on my own!" or the brush saying to the hand, "I will take it from here! I can make these perfect strokes. I don't need you anymore." We must be careful not to honor the creation over the Creator.

Walk with Him! Be blessed!

> God's word is alive and working. It is sharper than the sharpest sword and cuts all the way into us. It cuts deep to the place where the soul and the spirit are joined. God's word cuts to the center of our joints and our bones. It judges the thoughts and feelings in our hearts.

—Hebrews 4:12 (ERV)

Many years ago, when I was in the middle of a parenting meltdown, the Lord revealed something very important to me that has since been very helpful in many of my relationships with my family, my friends, and the young people I have taught and coached. It began like this: I was very frustrated from constantly having to tell my daughters to clean their rooms. I just didn't understand why they didn't want to do it. After all, if they understood how good a clean room was for them, then they would want to keep their room clean, right? It wasn't one of my finer moments as a parent. The Lord said (not audibly) something like, "You are getting frustrated at your girls and other people because you want them to want what is best for them. But know this: You can make your daughters make their bed, but you can't make them want to make their bed. You should mold their actions, and I will mold their hearts and attitudes. You do your part by being consistent. I will do My (the much more important) part by giving them the Word." It then dawned on me: it is so hard for people to make changes because they need to have the Word spoken into their lives constantly so it can be the double-edge sword that cuts to the marrow and makes them want to change. Wow!

When I gave up trying to change hearts and attitudes (which was never my job) and began to help people mold their actions by being consistent with my expectations, speaking the Word into their lives, and getting out of the way of the Holy Spirit's working in their individual lives, my frustrations subsided and I began to enjoy doing what I was called to do, that is, being a wife, mother, teacher, and friend who encourages those around me by speaking the Word with consistent expectations.

Walk with Him! Be blessed!

Oh give thanks to the Lord; call upon his name; make known his deeds among the peoples! Sing to him, sing praises to him; tell of all his wondrous works!

—Psalms 105:1–2 (ESV)

Give praise to God for the small things with which He blesses you daily. We live in a world that says that if something is not over the top, it isn't worth talking about. But the smallest movement of God is still much more than the most over-the-top thing in this world. Don't miss the everyday blessings of the Lord! Daily the sun rises, moves across the sky, and sets, all to bless you with another day. Praise and talk about Him who provides that to you. Walk with Him! Be blessed!

When he spoke before, his voice shook the earth. But now he has promised, "Once again I will shake the earth, but I will also shake heaven." The words "once again" clearly show us that everything that was created will be destroyed—that is, the things that can be shaken. And only what cannot be shaken will remain. So we should be thankful because we have a kingdom that cannot be shaken. And because we are thankful, we should worship God in a way that will please him. We should do this with respect and fear.

—Hebrews 12:26–28 (ERV)

This world can be shaken! From things like natural disasters to human-made chaos, this world is in constant turmoil. But those of us who have put our lives in the hands of the Creator through His Son can be thankful, because our kingdom cannot be shaken. Our time in this world is just a moment when compared to eternity (the unshakable kingdom). But until our eternity begins, we can be confident in the plans God has for us, no matter how shaken the world appears. Jeremiah 29:11 expresses a promise from God. It says to us, "'For I know the plans I have for you,' declares the Lord, 'plans to prosper you and not to harm you, plans to give you hope and a future.'" So until our unshakable kingdom comes, we can hold firm to the unshakable One. With a heart of thanksgiving, we can worship Him with fear (reverence) and respect in a manner that is pleasing to Him.

Walk with Him! Be blessed!

That's right because I, your God, have a firm grip on you and
I am not letting go. I am telling you don't panic! I am right
here to help you!

—Isaiah 41:13 (MSG)

Do you ever feel like you are hanging off the edge of a high cliff and your rope is on its last thread; that there is no way back up and the way down doesn't look too pleasant; that your arms are tired and almost numb from hanging on so long that you are about to give up and just let go, take the fall, and pray that the damage is not too great and that you will get by with a few bumps and bruises or a break or two; and that letting go would seem easier than continuing to hang on? Well, guess what? Even if you let go, God has you in His firm grip! And He is not letting go of you, not even if you let go of Him. Just look up and see who has a grip on you. Rest right there as you dangle from the side of your mountain. He will pull you up or lower you down. Either way, you are in His grip.

Walk with Him! Be blessed!

Do any of you need wisdom? Ask God for it. He is generous and enjoys giving to everyone. So he will give you wisdom. But when you ask God, you must believe. Don't doubt him. Whoever doubts is like a wave in the sea that is blown up and down by the wind. People like that are thinking two different things at the same time. They can never decide what to do. So they should not think they will receive anything from the Lord.

—James 1:5–8 (ERV)

It is interesting that this verse begins with a promise (namely, if you are lacking in wisdom, then just ask and you will receive, as the Lord is generous and loves to give) but ends with an admonishment (namely, you should not think that you will receive). Don't the beginning and the end cancel each other out? Just like in life, many times we see the beginning and know the desired end result, so that is where we put our focus—on where we are and where we want to be—only to miss the very important part of getting from one spot to the other. It is amid the journey where God wants to show Himself to us through our belief that He is able to do what He promises. Because of our disbelief or trust in His being able to get us from the beginning to the end, we get tossed around as if we were in the ocean and the high tide was coming in. Being in the high tide isn't the problem, though.

In John 16:33, Jesus says, "I have told you these things so in Me you will have peace. In this world you will have trouble but I have overcome this world." High tides will come in our lives, even when we have asked for direction. It is our double thinking that keeps us there and tosses us about longer than God intends. *Can I trust God, or can I not trust Him?* Thinking two things at the same time can keep us from seeing or hearing the very answers He has provided. It also prevents us from coming to know the reason we shouldn't expect to receive the very thing we are asking for. Christ understands our doubt, but He also knows who He is and knows He can be trusted.

Which is greater in your life, the knowledge of who Christ is and how He can be trusted; the doubt provided by the world; or your own impatience, which makes you question who He is? Maybe our doubt is where the tossing comes from and is what keeps us from experiencing the wisdom that God so generously gives. Belief or doubt: which is greater?

Walk with Him! Be blessed!

In the beginning was the Word, and the Word was with God, and the Word was God. He was in the beginning with God. All things were made through Him, and without him nothing came to be. In Him was life, and the life was the light of men. The light shines in the darkness, and the darkness has not overcome it.

—John 1:1–5 (ESV)

Jesus isn't a Band-Aid we apply when we have a wound and then take off when we are healed. Jesus is the Son of the Almighty God. He was with God when He spoke earth and life into being. Yes, Jesus heals us from our pain and sorrows and gives us peace that surpasses all understanding, but He is still the Lord God Almighty and deserves much more from the ones who have accepted His gift of eternal life through grace than to be applied only when needed. We need to remember we were in need of salvation, for which purpose He died, not a Band-Aid.

Walk with Him! Be blessed!

My brothers and sisters, you will have many kinds of trouble. But this gives you a reason to be very happy. You know that when your faith is tested, you learn to be patient in suffering my brothers and sisters, you will have many kinds of trouble. But this gives you a reason to be very happy. You know that when your faith is tested, you learn to be patient in suffering. If you let that patience work in you, the end result will be good. You will be mature and complete. You will be all that God wants you to be.

—James 1:2–4 (ERV)

In John 16:33 Jesus said, "I tell you these things so that you will have peace. In this world you will have trouble, but take heart I have overcome the world." The fact that this is repeated in the book of James shouldn't surprise us. Many things are repeated throughout Scripture, which must mean that God wants us to know what is being said. In John 16:33 Jesus tells us what He has done, namely, "overcome this world." In James 1:2–4 it tells us what we are to do, and that is to "be happy." Yep, it is said right there: "be happy" when your faith is tested, because (now for the results of the tested faith) you will learn patience in that suffering. And now for the conditional promise (geometry, which I teach, deals in if–then statements, so this I get!): if you let that patience work in you, then the end result will be good. You will be mature and complete. You will be all that God wants you to be, the key focus being on the "then" part. It is important to be mature and complete in Christ and to be what He wants us to be—not what we want to be, but what He wants us to be. If testing and suffering is what I need to become patient so I can become what He desires me to be, then I pray for a happy heart surrendered to that suffering, because to be what He desires is and should be my first desire above all others.

Walk with Him! Be blessed!

For just as the body is one and has many members, and all the members of the body, though many, are one body, so it is with Christ. For in one Spirit we were all baptized into one body—Jews or Greeks, slaves or free—and all were made to drink of one Spirit. For the body does not consist of one member but of many. If the foot should say, "Because I am not a hand, I do not belong to the body," that would not make it any less a part of the body. And if the ear should say, "Because I am not an eye, I do not belong to the body," that would not make it any less a part of the body. If the whole body were an eye, where would be the sense of hearing? If the whole body were an ear, where would be the sense of smell? But as it is, God arranged the members in the body, each one of them, as he chose. If all were a single member, where would the body be? As it is, there are many parts, yet one body. The eye cannot say to the hand, "I have no need of you," nor again the head to the feet, "I have no need of you." On the contrary, the parts of the body that seem to be weaker are indispensable, and on those parts of the body that we think less honorable we bestow the greater honor, and our unpresentable parts are treated with greater modesty, which our more presentable parts do not require. But God has so composed the body, giving greater honor to the part that lacked it, that there may be no division in the body, but that the members may have the same care for one another.

—1 Corinthians 12:12–25 (ESV)

These verses point to one of the biggest sins that most believers struggle with (because of the world we live in, in my opinion), and that is the art of comparing. As a matter of fact, making comparisons between believers has become a huge issue in the body of Christ, which is why I will discuss it in three parts.

First, I will talk about the comparison between the individual comparison and the world comparison, when we compare our life in Christ to a life in the world. If we aren't careful, we will begin to believe the lies the world tells, one of which is that a life in the world has much more to offer than a life in Christ does. Life in the world presents itself in a manner that makes us question if following Christ really has that much to offer and if it is really worth it in the end.

Yes, a life in Christ is worth it in the end, because the end is just the beginning for a believer. In Colossians 3:2–3, we are told to set our sights on things above, where Christ Jesus sits at the right hand of God the Father. This world will pass away, and those whose hope is in it will pass away too. But those who have put their trust in Christ have the promise of an eternity with Him. In John 14:3 Jesus said, "I go to my Father to prepare for you a place and at the right time, I will return for you where then you will be with me." No matter what the world seems to offer, it pales in comparison to the eternity we are promised.

Second, the art of comparison causes struggles in one's walk with Christ when an individual believer compares herself to another individual believer. Like it says in the verses above, we tend to look at the talent, gifts, or position of others compared to our own, and then we start ranking them in order of importance according to our ranking system. We think that what is seen must be more important than what isn't seen. The hand has to have more importance than the bottom of the foot, right? Similarly, the voice is even more important than the hand because it demands attention when it speaks. When we look at ourselves as individual parts of a body, it is easy for us to compare and to start seeing one part as more important than another, which causes us not to value or use the part of the body we have deemed less valuable.

What happens when a part of the body is not exercised or cared for properly? It becomes weak and the purpose it was created for becomes compromised. But that isn't the only harm being caused. The part that is being overused is also harmed, as it becomes weakened and damaged because of the overuse. The body, just like the body of individual believers, is created to work together for the glory of Christ, not to compete for importance. Whether we are the person who shares the gospel with one individual or the person who shares it with thousands, whether we offer a meal to one person or to a whole city of people, whether we bandage one knee or give medicine to an entire country, we are all a part of one body created to bring God the Father glory.

Third, the art of comparison has also become a stumbling block when considering a church-to-church comparison. Much like the churches (the groups of people who believed in Christ) in the New Testament, we begin to look at what another group is or isn't doing and compare it with what we are or aren't doing. We also begin to evaluate how those other groups may be missing the mark. Unfortunately, this becomes not only a comparison game but also a competition between churches (groups of people). When competition takes place, at some point one party is declared the winner while all the rest are declared losers. If certain body parts, all of which are created and designed to work beautifully together, compete with other body parts, then the body becomes unhealthy, just like the body of believers. This is why a metaphor has been used in the verses above, to get us to understand how the church has been designed. It could be explained like this: When designing the body, God was very creative. The body is very intricate and has many different parts. The three things needed no matter where an organ is located in the body, are blood, oxygen, and the heart, which makes sure all parts receive these blood and oxygen to stay alive. Christ is the blood that all parts must have to function as they are designed to function. The Holy Spirit (oxygen) must be brought by the blood (Christ) to all the body parts. And it is the heart (God) that continues to pump the blood (Christ) filled with oxygen (Holy Spirit) to all parts of the body, as blood and oxygen are things that all of the body parts need to be healthy, and to function as they are designed to function. If we can focus on all the body parts, even though some may be different, and see that all are fed from the same source with the same blood flow, then we will begin to see the body as a whole and not as separate parts that must compete to live. This way, we will be a life source for others.

> But if it seems wrong in your opinion to serve the Lord, then choose today whom you will serve. Choose the gods whom your ancestors served beyond the Euphrates or the gods of the Amorites in whose land you live. But my family and I will still serve the Lord.

—Joshua 24:15 (CEB)

A favorite quotation I use when encouraging young people to make wise choices is, "Don't expect A-plus results when making D-minus choices." I found it interesting when I gave this advice to someone and then the above verse came to my mind. The words that jumped out were *want* and *choose*, which made me think a little deeper. Before I accepted Christ's gift of salvation and eternity, I didn't really have any choices to choose from. I was a slave to my sin, which was highly influenced by my selfish wants, much like the Israelites when living in bondage to Egypt, as they didn't have the freedom to make many choices. It was only after they had been brought out of the chains of slavery they had been living under that they began to have a choice of how to live. Yet so many times they kept turning back, "choosing" the very chains they had been set free from. Too many times, those of us who have been set free and who are now walking in the promises of our Lord and Savior (like the Israelites in the Promised Land) choose something other than what we have received through our salvation. We *choose* to walk in the ways of what we previously have known. We *choose* to walk in the ways of the world we live in. I can only speak for myself when addressing these choices. The reason I once made them is that I preferred my selfish wants over service to the Lord. With the gift of salvation comes the gift of choice: whom one will serve. I now choose to walk in the new life I have received. It is because of this that I *choose* to serve the Lord.

Walk with Him! Be blessed!

When you are praying and you remember that you are angry with another person about something, forgive that person. Forgive them so that your Father in heaven will also forgive your sins.

—Mark 11:25 (ERV)

So, what if you are offering your gift at the altar and remember that someone has something against you? Leave your gift there and go make peace with that person. Then come and offer your gift.

—Matthew 5:23–24 (ERV)

In the verses above, we are told to forgive. We are also told to ask for others' forgiveness. Why is it so important that we forgive and be forgiven by others? Because of the direct impact forgiveness has on our relationship with our Lord and Savior. If we know we have offended or wronged someone and haven't yet asked to be forgiven, and if we simultaneously desire to approach the Lord with our gifts and talents, then He tells us to go make peace with that person before returning to Him. Why? Because asking forgiveness helps us understand how to walk in peace with Him. When we have offended someone and we then ask for forgiveness, and when we see our relationship with that person become better as a result, it helps us to understand the forgiveness we receive from Christ. If another human can forgive me, then how much more can the God of the universe forgive?

The first verse tell us to be the forgiver. Note that it doesn't say we should forgive someone if and when that person asks for our forgiveness. It just says, essentially, "When you are praying and are angry with someone, forgive that person." It doesn't advise us to ask the Lord to fix someone so we can forgive him or her. It doesn't say to ask the Lord to give us an apology from a person who has offended us. It says that we must forgive others. Why? Once again, doing so will improve our relationship with the Lord. To offer unconditional forgiveness to another, whether the person asks for it or not, whether the relationship is ever restored or not, and whether the mercy is deserved or undeserved, helps us to understand how our Lord can give us unconditional forgiveness. So whether we are talking about being forgiven or giving forgiveness, it is not only the human-to-human relationship that is affected by forgiveness. Our relationship with our Lord and Savior is also affected. Walk with Him! Be blessed!

Take Delight in the Lord and he will give you the desires of your heart.

—Psalms 37:4 (NIV)

This verse doesn't mean that if you get happy with Jesus, you will get what you want. (Unfortunately, many people think that this is the meaning.) Another verse in the Bible says it this way: "Commit your work to the Lord, and your plans will be established" (Proverbs 16:3 ESV). That is, if you commit yourself to God, then your plans will become known (in other words, God's desires will become known to you). What He desires for you will become, through your commitment to Him, what you desire to do. This thought brings me to the verse in Proverbs 16:9: "In his heart a man plans his path but the Lord determines his steps." Many times, a desire or direction is been placed in our hearts that truly is from God. This is not a desire for self but a desire that is from Him, because it requires something from us that—without the directive being from Him—we wouldn't or couldn't do on our own.

If you are like me, you start planning out how something honoring God can come to be. *How I can make this happen?* I get all the details in place and am ready to get started on the project of making these desires placed in my heart by God come to pass. And being a geometry teacher, I totally understand what it takes to get from point A to point B. I understand that the shortest distance between any two points is a perpendicular line (if you aren't sure what that is, look it up). I am ready to roll! As a matter of fact, if I could, I would just fly to point B. Flying is faster and safer than driving, correct? But wait. The Lord doesn't even want me to drive on the path that has been established by Him. He wants me to walk! And He will determine my steps. "But, Lord, I've got it. I know where we are going, and I want to get there fast. I want so much to do this for You, Lord!"

To this, He replies, "Walk with Me! I have things along this path you are going to need when you get to where we are going. You will only have the wisdom, the understanding, and most importantly the love by spending time with Me walking." So if the Lord has placed a desire in your heart or has given you insight into His plans and yet you don't seem to be getting closer to what you know you are called to do, don't panic, don't give up, and don't take a different path. Just know that you are moving in the direction He is taking you as you walk with Him.

God's way is perfect. The Lord's promise always proves to be true. He protects those who trust in him. There is no God except the Lord. There is no Rock except our God. God is my strong fortress. He clears the path I need to take. He makes my feet as steady as those of a deer. Even on steep mountains he keeps me from falling.

—Samuel 22:31–34 (ERV)

If you have ever seen a mountain goat on the side of a mountain, then you know it is a pretty incredible sight. Mountain goats in such a position look like they are standing on air with no place to go. And how do they even turn around to go in any direction? I know that my distance from the goat distorts the view of the actual topography the goat is standing on, but still it amazes me. How do mountain goats get up that high to begin with? The answer might be found in the verses above. The mountain goats are doing what they were created to do, and that is to live on the rocky and steep sides of mountains. They keep climbing to new heights because they know they are designed to do just that, just like we have been designed for a relationship with the Almighty God. Through His perfection, He designed a way for us to know His promises through His Son, Jesus Christ. These promises have been proven to be true. This has been done so we can bring glory and praise to Him and come to know Him as the one true God. We come to know the God who is the Rock of our salvation and our strong fortress. Therefore, no matter where we walk on the path, we know that our path is steady, even on the rockiest and steepest slopes, because we have the assurance that we are doing what we have been designed for—and that is to walk in a relationship with God no matter the terrain. Walk with Him! Be blessed!

Let us, then, always offer praise to God as our sacrifice through Jesus, which is the offering presented by lips that confess him as Lord. Do not forget to do good and to help one another, because these are the sacrifices that please God.

—Hebrews 13:15–16 (GNT)

May what we say and do today give our heavenly Father a reason to smile on His children as we honor Jesus with our words and actions.

Walk with Him! Be blessed!

Whoever has my commands and keeps them is the one who loves me. The one who loves me will be loved by my Father, and I too will love them and show myself to them.

—John 14:21 (NIV)

When I read this verse and see the words *commands* and *keeps*, my first thought is of the Ten Commandments from the Old Testament. But Jesus took those ten and rolled them into these two: (1) love the Lord your God with all you have, and (2) love your neighbor as yourself. (Keep these is mind.) Many times I want to see and know God's presence in my life. I ask and ask almost to the point of being demanding (this is not Christlike; it is childlike). Sometimes I even let Him know how He should show me His presence (very arrogant of me, I know!). If certain situations work out how I want them to, then I let Him know ("Now I know You are present in my life"). (I definitely need prayer!) Unfortunately in these times, I am totally missing the point. "Whoever keeps these commands [the amazing two mentioned above] is the one who loves me!" To know God's presence, I must first show my love for Him by loving Him with everything I have. Then I must love others as I so selfishly love myself. "The one who loves me will be loved by my Father and I too will love them and show myself to them." So basically I need to get over myself and get onto loving God, Christ, and others. Then I won't have to ask to be shown the presence of Christ in my life, as it will be shown to me in ways I wouldn't even know how to ask for!

Walk with Him! Be blessed!

For as the heavens are higher than the earth, so are my ways higher than your ways and my thoughts than your thoughts.

—Isaiah 55:9 (ESV)

Hooray for new running shoes! Don't get me wrong, I was very comfortable in my old pair that had about seven thousand miles clocked on them, but only after I put on a new pair and ran in them did I realize how worn down the other pair was. I bought a new pair only because I thought it was time to, not because I thought something was wrong with the other pair. But now that I have put on the new pair, I realize that I probably should have gotten a new pair about two hundred miles ago. Does that speak to you like it does to me? How many times do I keep doing, thinking, and living in the same way long past the time I should, especially considering that God's Word clearly tells me to renew my mind daily? I go through the motions of reading the Word, praying, praising God, and following my daily routine, yet I am just putting on the same ol' shoes and not even realizing I need a new pair. God's Word is always fresh and always new! That is how it has lasted, and that is how it continues to make a difference in this world. Daily I need to remember that God's ways are not my ways. His ways are fresh and new daily. I need to come to Him expecting a daily run with new shoes on my feet.

His ways are new daily! Walk with Him! Be blessed!

So the Lord is waiting to show his mercy to you. He wants to rise and comfort you. The Lord is the God who does the right thing, so he will bless everyone who waits for his help.

—Isaiah 30:18 (ERV)

The last line of this verse contains a promise from God. It says that we will receive a blessing when we wait on Him. There is a lot more to this verse than the idea that we will be blessed if we wait on the Lord. Let's start with the word *so*. *So*, being at the beginning of the verse, indicates that there is something before that this verse is connected to. So let's read those verses, beginning with 15 and ending with 17:

> The Lord God, the Holy One of Israel, says, "If you come back to me you will be saved. Only by remaining calm and trusting in me can you be strong." But you don't want to do that. You say, "No, we need fast horses for battle." That is true—you will need fast horses, but only to run away because your enemy will be faster than your horses. One enemy soldier will make threats, and a thousand of your men will run away. And when five of them make threats, all of you will run away. The only thing that will be left of your army will be a flagpole on a hill. (Isaiah 30:15–17 ERV)

God begins by saying, "If you come back to me," which means that (1) we have a choice and (2) we aren't where we need to be if we are to trust in Him to remain calm and strong—because we are told we need to return to Him. Then the verse reads, "But you don't want to." Ouch! His Word then tells us that we aren't listening to Him. We are too busy telling Him what we need to have in order to fight this fight and the way we think it should be fought (i.e., we need fast horses). He then responds with, "Yes, if you do it your way, you will need fast horses, but only to continue running away from what you are facing! So when you are ready to wait on Me, then you will be ready to see and experience My mercies, comfort, and blessings."

This is great stuff, but I often struggle with these things. I am not always patient, I want a quick resolution to things, and I spend too much time telling my Lord and Savior what I need and what I hope the outcome of something will be. All the while He is waiting on me to just wait and trust in Him. Second Peter 3:9 reminds us that the Lord is not being slow in doing what He promised—the way some people understand slowness—but that He is being patient with us. He doesn't want anyone to be lost. He wants everyone to change their ways and to trust in Him. I need to just walk with Him and be blessed!

But now put these things out of your life: anger, losing your temper, doing or saying things to hurt others, and saying shameful things.

—Colossians 3:8 (ERV)

A young man, a student of mine, had a cool Christian sweatshirt. I had seen him wear it two times, and both times I told him how cool it was. Toward the end of class one day, I heard him talking about a fight he'd had with his parents. He said he had yelled at them and they had yelled back, and then he walked out on them. He just wasn't going to put up with them. And before I knew it, I said, "So did you have that sweatshirt on while all this was going on?" Oops! But, really, how often are we willing to put on the clothing, to put on an outward show, of being a follower of Christ while simultaneously feeling justified in not acting like one when we don't agree with someone or something that has happened, all the while wearing our Jesus shirt or a cross around our neck? The saddest part is this: people don't just see us in these situations. They see Jesus as less than who He is because of us. There is a saying (one I am not too fond of, really), "You might be the only Jesus someone sees." Wow! Think on that a while.

Walk with Him! Be blessed!

If we say we live in God, we must live the way Jesus lived.

—1 John 2:6 (ERV)

I love when I see a Bible verse displayed on a car, a shirt, a tattoo, or someplace else. I immediately look it up to see what the person who has it displayed wants others to know. And I have to say that the verse above seemed like something impossible to do after I read it on a bumper sticker on a truck. Live like Jesus! Wow, but how? How can I heal people, feed thousands of people, and do all the other miraculous things Christ did? Isn't this what it means if I am to live like Him? How can a forgiven sinner live and do like Christ, the Son of God, lived and did? I can't. He was God in the flesh.. But the reason Christ did all those things was so that I can too. He lived and died on the cross, yes, for our salvation, but even more so to bring honor and glory to God, His Father. And that I can do too. First Corinthians 10:31 reads, "So whether you eat or drink or whatever you do, do it all for the glory of God." This means that my life isn't so much about what I do but why I do it: to bring honor and glory to God the Father. Do I fail sometimes? Yes. Unlike Christ, who is unblemished, I am flawed, but I can live as Jesus instructed us to live when He said, "The greatest commandment is to love the Lord your God with all your heart, your mind, and your soul. And the second is to love your neighbor as you love yourself." And with that I can live like Christ, in everything I do bringing honor and glory to the Father.

Walk with Him! Be blessed!

> Similarly, anyone who competes as an athlete does not receive the victor's crown except by competing according to the rules.
>
> —2 Timothy 2:5 (NIV)

What I am about to say may or may not be connected to this verse, but since the difference between losing and being beaten was on my mind, I found the New Testament verse that mentions competing. I don't mind getting beaten, but I can barely handle losing. What is the difference? To me, being beaten means that everything was done to set up my opponent for the win and that he or she was just better than I or made the right play at the right time. My opponent's success doesn't take away from my work, my preparation, my dedication. I didn't lose; I just got beaten. On the other hand, losing means that I didn't do the things needed to set me up for victory. The other team or individual wasn't necessarily better than I or didn't simply make the right play at the right time.

Losing reveals your work, your preparation, and your dedication. Just like in life, if you get "beaten out" for a job or new position, it doesn't take away from the qualities you possess, from the work you have done, or from the time and energy you have invested in the opportunity. It doesn't reflect on who you are. On the other hand, if you *lose* an opportunity because of how you prepared, because the time you invested wasn't sufficient or of the right quality, or because the work you did wasn't what was needed for the opportunity, then that does reflect on who you are. There is good news, though! At any point we can begin to do things differently. And if we do change our ways, then who knows what might happen? We might come out with the victor's crown in a sport or, better yet, in life. If we don't, at least we know we didn't lose—we just got beaten!

Walk with Him! Be blessed!

Lord, be kind to us. We have waited for your help. Give us strength every morning. Save us when we are in trouble.

—Isaiah 33:2 (ERV)

My friend Gina shared this verse with me. Thanks to her for reminding us that the Lord is our strength. He is the one who sees us through the trials of our daily lives, and He is gracious to us through it all. Why wouldn't we long for more of Him in our lives when we really come to know Him as our salvation? Walk with Him! Be blessed!

Shadrach, Meshach, and Abednego answered King Nebuchadnezzar, "Your threat means nothing to us. If you throw us in the fire, the God we serve can rescue us from your roaring furnace and anything else you might cook up, O king. But even if he doesn't, it wouldn't make a bit of difference, O king. We still wouldn't serve your gods or worship the gold statue you set up."

—Daniel 3:16–18 (MSG)

People need Jesus! He is whom we are born to seek, find, and glorify. Yet sometimes in our desire to point others to Him, we make Him out to be less than who He is. The same thing happens when we turn people to Him only when they are in a time of a need. We present Him as the great fixer of our problems instead of who He is—and that is the Son of God. People do need Jesus, but not just so He can fix our problems. We need Him because we are created for Him (instead of Him being created for us). Yes, He did come to die on the cross for our sins, but it wasn't just for our salvation. It was also to bring glory to the Father! Christ could have called the angels to take Him off the cross, which would have definitely fixed the situation He was in and brought a lot of awe and glory to Him, but He chose to do not His will but the Father's will.

Shadrach, Meshach, and Abednego most definitely needed a fix in their lives. They were about to be thrown into an intense fire. Yet they said, essentially, "Our God can save us from this problem. But even if He chooses not to take us out of this fire, we won't look for a different solution to our situation, because our faith is in who He is, not just in what He can or will do for us." When our faith is grounded in who Christ is, we come to understand that our solution could, and probably will, look much different from what we might be asking for.

Walk with Him! Be blessed!

The Lord himself will go ahead of you, He will be with you. He will never leave you. He'll never desert you. So don't be afraid. Don't lose hope.

—Deuteronomy 31:8 (NIRV)

Wow, oh wow, what a great promise for today, tomorrow, or years down the road. We have no clue what today, tomorrow, or this year will bring, but we do have the promise that God our Father has already gone before us! He has walked the path we will walk, and now He comes back to get us so as to walk it with us—and then He goes back to follow us. He knows every hill, every valley, every twist, every turn. Do not be discouraged or afraid. Go boldly and walk with Him! Be blessed!

Jesus healed many during His time on earth. There were times the crowd was so thick around Him people cut holes in the roof to get people with physical needs close to Him! Since they could not get him to Jesus because of the crowd, they made an opening in the roof above Jesus by digging through it and then lowered the mat the man was lying on.

—Mark 2:4 (ESV)

There was the woman who knew she needed just a touch of Christ to heal her. She had heard the reports about Jesus and came up behind him in the crowd and touched his garment. For she said, "If I touch even his garments, I will be made well."

—Mark 5:27–28 (ESV)

Much of Jesus's time during His three years of declaring who He is was spent healing the sick and comforting the downtrodden. Jesus also took care of the physical needs of thousands by feeding them after He multiplied fives loaves of bread and two fish. "Jesus then took the loaves, and when he had given thanks, he distributed them to those who were seated. So also the fish, as much as they wanted" (John 6:11 ESV). Today we encourage many to come to Christ because He can help with the many needs of this life. Christ is the Great Physician, but He is the Son of God first and foremost. We must be careful not to let our needs get in the way of knowing Him as who He is, and that is the Son of the Trinity. "For God so loved the world He sent His only Son that who so ever believes in Him shall not perish but have eternal life!" John 3:16 reminds us who Christ is first and foremost, the One sent by God to reconcile us to God Himself! Yes, Christ meets our needs, but even if our needs aren't met, or if they are met differently than we desire, it doesn't change who He is, namely, the Son of the living God. Walk with Him! Be blessed!

Do not be anxious about anything, but in everything by prayer and supplication with thanksgiving let your requests be made known to God. And the peace of God, which surpasses all understanding, will guard your hearts and your minds in Christ Jesus.

—Philippians 4:6–7 (ESV)

Whatever today holds, be reminded that it has already passed by and through your heavenly Father and your Savior, the latter of whom is sitting at the former's right hand interceding for you. And with that, you can truly do *all* things through Christ, who strengthens you! I believe that "And we know that in all things God works for the good of those who love Him, who have been called according to His purpose." (Romans 8:28 NIV). This doesn't mean that we will get what we want, but it does mean that if we will truly trust our heavenly Father and the One who died for us no matter what happens, our relationship with Them will grow closer and we will become more of what God desires us to be. Only through our relationship with Christ can we experience the peace that passes *all* understanding. Just because this world is crazy doesn't mean that we have to be.

Walk with Him! Be blessed!

For God loved the world so much that he gave his only Son, so that everyone who believes in him may not die but have eternal life. For God did not send his Son into the world to be its judge, but to be its savior.

—John 3:16–17 (GNT)

The gospel of Jesus is simple: accept Christ as your Lord and Savior, and eternity with Him is yours. Yet we keep trying to make it complicated, thinking we need to add something to it. On the other hand, we keep trying to make life simple when it is actually complicated and messy. Jesus even told us, "I have told you this so that you will have peace by being united to me. The world will make you suffer. But be brave! I have defeated the world" (John 16:33 GNT)! We want life to be easy, rosy, and uncomplicated, but it isn't. When it isn't, we begin to look at Christ differently, even though in His Word we are told that life will be messy.

How do we live in the simplicity of the promises of Christ without getting confused by the messiness of life? "If then you have been raised with Christ, seek the things that are above, where Christ is, seated at the right hand of God. Set your minds on things that are above, not on things that are on earth" (Colossians 3:1–2 ESV). Our sight, not just of our eyes but also of our heart, mind, and soul, must stay focused on Christ. Also, we must hold to His promises that are written throughout Scriptures, for example, Hebrews 13:14: "For this world is not our home; we are looking forward to our city in heaven, which is yet to come." Life is messy, but we are never alone in the mess.

Walk with Him! Be blessed!

For God so loved the world He gave His one and only Son, that whosoever believes in Him shall not perish, but have eternal life.

—John 3:16 (NIV)

Warning: if you continue reading, you might be offended by what I say. If you are still reading, know you have been warned! We have become such a people of entitlement, thinking we deserve more than what we have. We believe that life is not fair because we don't get what we think we deserve. I now understand that I should be thankful when I don't receive what I deserve, which is death and eternal separation from the one true righteous and holy God, because of my sin. But because He is loving, He sent His one and only Son, Christ, to earth to die on the cross for me—and for anyone else who will accept Him as Savior and Lord—so I don't ever have to be separated from Him, not during my time on earth or in eternity. I am very thankful that I don't get what I deserve! Thank you, Jesus! My prayer is that I will live to say "Thank you" to Him who paid the price so I can always walk with Him. Be blessed!

Above all, be careful what you think because your thoughts control your life. Don't bend the truth or say things that you know are not right.

—Proverbs 4:23–24 (ERV)

"Be careful what you think because your thoughts control your life" can also mean that your thoughts control your emotions. The verse above begins with, "Above all." When you read what is written before these verses (and I do encourage you to read Proverbs 4:1–22, as there is some really good stuff in there), you find that we are instructed, above all things, to make sure we know we are able do what it is we are called to do. We need to know how our thoughts (emotions) play into it. Many times we say, "Lord, I give You control," because we want the burdens of life to be lifted. We want to walk in the freedom we know comes from Christ, so we say, "Here, Lord, take it!" We let go for a while, and then what do we do? We start thinking again. Thoughts of our past, our present, and our future, sometimes slowly and sometimes quickly, begin consuming us. The next thing we know, those thoughts are controlling our lives.

It is kind of like this: we can do things to lose weight. If we follow a program of exercise and eat proper servings of healthy foods, we will lose weight. But as soon as we have reached our goal and we stop following the program, what happens a lot of the time? Far too quickly the weight returns. Why? Because we go back to our old way of thinking about food and exercise. We tried to change our weight by changing our actions before we changed our thoughts about our actions! How do we get past our thoughts and move back into the promises of Proverbs 4:1–22? Second Corinthians 10:4–5 (ERV) reads, "The weapons we use are not human ones. Our weapons have power from God and can destroy the enemy's strong places. We destroy people's arguments, and we tear down every proud idea that raises itself against the knowledge of God. We also capture every thought and make it give up and obey Christ." If we truly want to change our lives, then we must first give up our thoughts to Christ. Romans 12:2 reminds us, "Do not conform to the pattern of this world, but be transformed by the renewing of your mind. Then you will be able to test and approve what God's will is—his good, pleasing and perfect will." We must be in the Word daily so it can renew our minds so He, in turn, can renew us.

Walk with Him! Be blessed!

Lean on, trust in, and be confident in the Lord with all your heart and mind and do not rely on your own insight or understanding. In all your ways know, recognize, and acknowledge Him, and He will direct and make straight and plain your paths.

—Proverbs 3:5–6 (AB)

On our way back from Woodward, Oklahoma, to Borger, Texas, my husband, Ted, said something very thought-provoking. It went something like this: "There are many things I wouldn't think about doing at my age, like bungee jumping or getting in one of those sling chairs, yet I will get in a car and drive seventy-five miles an hour [the legal speed limit in Texas on two-lane roads] and pass someone I do not know who is within six feet of me and doing the same thing while going in the opposite direction, fully trusting that person to stay in his or her lane!"

I immediately thought, *This is so true. We are willing to do this quite often, yet I struggle with trusting Christ!* I trust people in cars driving (what appears to be) straight at me at times. Even though I have not been given the opportunity to meet these people, I give them my trust. I don't pull over to the side of the road and wait until they pass. I don't call them up and ask them, "Are you sure you can handle driving in that lane?" Nope, I just keep driving, because I "trust" them. Hmm, if I can trust someone I don't even know, how much more should I be able trust the One who lived, died, and rose to give me eternal life so that each day I can walk in the newness of life? How much more should I trust the One who created this very thing I get to live every day, life? I realize that many times I do, in effect, pull over to the side of the road and question Him about what He is able to do, ask Him if He really knows the road ahead and if He can handle it, and ask Him if I can really trust Him!

Driving or riding in a car has now taken on a whole new meaning.

Walk with Him! Be blessed!

I wait for the Lord, my soul waits, and in his word I hope; my soul waits for the Lord more than watchmen wait for the morning.

—Psalms 130:5–6 (ESV)

In today's world of hustle and bustle, we have become very impatient, wanting immediate answers and fixes. We want it now! Unfortunately, that causes us not to walk with God and patiently wait on His perfect timing in our lives. (Remember Sarah and Abraham and their unwillingness to wait on the Lord? If you don't remember, check out the Old Testament. Their story is in there.)

I pose a challenge to you: don't hurry today. Slow down and wait on the goodness of God to be shown to you, and then praise and thank Him, the One who died for you. Walk with Him! Be blessed!

Thy word have I hid in mine heart, that I might not sin against thee.

—Psalms 119:11 (KJV)

This is one of my favorite verses. I have always found the meaning to be something like this: "I have hidden Your Word in my heart, so Your Word will be just what I do." I am a firm believer in repetition when it comes to learning, so the more I hear, study, and apply the Word, the more it should become who I am. But I believe that the Lord cautioned me about my approach. It might seem great that the Word becomes just what you do, but be careful about hiding it so deep in your heart that you forget why you do what you do, which is to bring praise, honor, and glory to God, your heavenly Father, your Savior, your Lord! Wow! It is kind of like this: I can teach people to do math and even get them to be pretty good at it by showing them to follow the steps. I call this knowing the mechanics of math. I can teach people how to make math work for them even if they aren't quite sure why it works. But those few people who get not only the mechanics of math but also the why seem to be able to enjoy math much more than those who do it just to get it done enjoy it.

Be careful to prevent God's good and perfect Word from becoming "mechanical" in you by not coming to understand why it is in your life: all for His glory.

Walk with Him! Be blessed!

But keep the Lord Christ holy in your hearts. Always be ready to answer everyone who asks you to explain about the hope you have. But answer them in a gentle way with respect. Keep your conscience clear. Then people will see the good way you live as followers of Christ, and those who say bad things about you will be ashamed of what they said.

—1 Peter 3:15–16 (ERV)

Psalms 119:11 reads, "I have hidden Your Word in my heart so that I will not sin against You, O Lord." Here is another reason we should "hide" the Word in our hearts: so when we are asked to explain our hope, we can. But if the Word is hidden in our heart, how will people know to ask about the hope we have? By the way we live hope-filled lives! This world is crazy, but we don't have to be. This world is filled with fear, but we don't need to be. This world is critical and looking to tear people and things down, but we can be uplifting, loving, and kind, even in disagreement. In other words: don't look like the world! Then when people ask where your hope comes from, you won't have to search for your answer. You'll just respond from the heart, where the answer has been waiting to be shared.

Walk with Him! Be blessed!

The Son was there before anything was made. And all things continue because of him. He is the head of the body, which is the church. He is the beginning of everything else. And he is the first among all who will be raised from death. So in everything he is most important.

—Colossians 1:17–18 (ERV)

There's gotta be something more
Gotta be more than this
I need a little less hard time
I need a little more bliss
I'm gonna take my chances
Taking a chance I might
Find what I'm looking for
There's gotta be something more.[1]

Those lyrics are from a catchy tune released a few years back, but they still offer a relevant message about the world today. The problem with the message is that once we have found today's "more," the world changes it up on us tomorrow—but the "more" has been with us since the beginning of creation. "In the beginning was the Word and the Word was with God and the Word was God" (John 1:1 NIV). Let's not forget the promise of, "I will never leave you never will I forsake you" (Hebrews 13:5 NIV), along with the many other promises we have in the Word.

Why do we keep looking for the something more out of life? Maybe because we have accepted Christ as our Savior but have not given Him *lordship* of our lives, where He is everything, where He is most important.

Walk with Him! Be blessed!

---

[1] "Something More," Sugarland, *Twice the Speed of Life.* Mercury Records B0002172-02, 2005, compact disc.

Complain if you must, but don't lash out. Keep your mouth shut, and let your heart do the talking. Build your case before God and wait for his verdict.

—Psalms 4:4–5 (MSG)

I love how this verse tells us to talk with our hearts and to keep our mouths shut. This may be because our mouths are an extension of our thoughts and our heart are an expression of our spirit. Have you felt the turmoil and struggle between your thoughts and your heart, where your thoughts are pulling you one way and your heart is pulling you another? In Romans 7:15, Paul says, "For what I am doing, I do not understand; for I am not practicing what I would like to do, but I am doing the very thing I hate." Why do we still experience this struggle when we have the promise of becoming a new creation when we give our lives to Christ? "Wherefore if any man is in Christ, he is a new creature: the old things are passed away; behold, they are become new" (2 Corinthians 5:17 ASV). I heard it explained this way: when we surrender to Christ, the spirit inside of us—the real person inside the bag of bones we call the body—is renewed. Our brains are still flesh and blood, keeping a record of everything we have ever done. Our spirit is new, but we still have lost minds. Therein lies the conflict!

The Word is very important in this constant battle between the old mind and the new creation Christ has breathed life into. In Romans 12:2 we are told, "Do not conform to the pattern of this world, but be transformed by the renewing of your mind. Then you will be able to test and approve what God's will is—his good, pleasing and perfect will." Renewal implies a continual process. In Psalms 4, we are told to speak with our heart (the new spirit given to us by Christ) and not our mouths. The battle for our spirit has been won! The battle of our mind is ongoing and is won daily by God's Word in our life. Walk with Him! Be blessed!

The truly happy person doesn't follow wicked advice, doesn't stand on the road of sinners, and doesn't sit with the disrespectful. Instead of doing those things, these persons love the Lord's Instruction, and they recite God's Instruction day and night! They are like a tree replanted by streams of water, which bears fruit at just the right time and whose leaves don't fade. Whatever they do succeeds.

—Psalms 1:1–3 (CEB)

If I understand the above verse correctly, I believe it is saying that we shouldn't leave our house if we want to be truly happy. We are instructed not to follow the advice of the wicked, but the advice of the wicked is readily available; you get the advice whether you want it or not. When we are advised not to stand on the road of sinners, I ask myself, *Well, isn't everyone a sinner? So do we avoid all people?* When we are instructed not to sit with people who are disrespectful, I see that disrespect is as common as sin (the two are actually the same), so where do we go to avoid disrespectful people. Hmm, maybe what is being said is this: "Don't follow the advice of the wicked" doesn't mean that we won't hear foolish advice. Instead, as it says later in the verses above, we must know and love the Word of God, which will help us to know the difference between the advice of the foolish and the instructions of God. Knowing the difference will enable us not to follow the advice of the foolish. To not stand on the road of sinners or sit with the disrespectful doesn't mean that we are never to come into contact with sinners or disrespectful people, or separate ourselves out to the point that we are not able to share the message of Christ. What it could mean is that we shouldn't plant ourselves in the midst of disrespectful sinners but that we should, instead, be replanted by the stream of life, which is Christ. In others words, Christ should be what is watering us so that our lives look different from the lives of those who aren't planted by the stream. This doesn't make us better than others, but it does make us different, because our Source of life is the living water of Christ and not the things of this world.

Walk with Him! Be blessed!

Don't worry—I am with you. Don't be afraid—I am your God. I will make you strong and help you. I will support you with my right hand that brings victory.

—Isaiah 41:10 (ERV)

I am the Lord your God, who holds your right hand. And I tell you, "Don't be afraid! I will help you."

—Isaiah 41:13 (ERV)

I love that in Isaiah 41:10 God assures us He is with us and making us strong. He is supporting us with His right hand. He is bringing us to victory. Then, in verse 13, He says, "I am the Lord your God. I have you! Let your fear go. I am with you!" God knows we need to be reassured often of His faithfulness, kindness, strength, protection, and guidance, and of His undying and forever love. He has no problem repeating Himself in His Word so that we can grow in our faith and trust in who He is. Walk with Him! Be blessed!

So we will wait for the Lord. He helps us and protects us.

—Psalms 33:20 (ERV)

Aw, there is the ol' *wait* word. Man, it is mentioned often throughout God's Word. Why is it so important for us to learn patience, to learn to wait on the Lord? In Isaiah 40:31 we are told, "But they that wait upon the Lord shall renew their strength; they shall mount up with wings as eagles; they shall run, and not be weary; and they shall walk, and not faint." Maybe He is desiring us to learn patience because He is so patient with us. Psalms 103:8 it reads, "The Lord is kind and merciful. He is patient and full of love." Maybe this is so we can see the difference between God and this hectic, fast-paced world. Whatever it is, we are encouraged and told to wait on the Lord many, many times in His Word. And if He tells us to do something, He provides the way to do it. So when you are waiting on the Lord and you begin to feel like you just can't wait any longer, know that you can. Why? Because He tells us to wait on Him. And because He tells us to means that we can.

Walk with Him! Be blessed!

Brothers and sisters, God chose you to be his. Think about that! Not many of you were wise in the way the world judges wisdom. Not many of you had great influence, and not many of you came from important families. But God chose the foolish things of the world to shame the wise. He chose the weak things of the world to shame the strong. And God chose what the world thinks is not important—what the world hates and thinks is nothing. He chose these to destroy what the world thinks is important. God did this so that no one can stand before him and boast about anything.

—1 Corinthians 1:26–29 (ERV)

Man, these verses can be a boost to your ego and make you feel pretty special because you are in the group God chooses to use, or they can be a blow to your ego because you are in the group God chooses to use. Look whom it says He chooses to use: the unwise, the uninfluential who come from unimportant families, the foolish, the weak, the hated of the world, and those who are seen as nothing in the world. Ouch! But it hurts only if these verses are read from the world's point of view. The last sentence says it all! "God did this so no one can stand before Him and boast about anything!" This means no one, whether you are important in the world or being used by God. Nothing we do gives us a reason to stand before God and boast. This is because being used by God isn't about us at all. It is all about Christ and what He did. To be used by God is very humbling, and to know He chooses to use us even when we aren't qualified to be used is even more humbling. Walk with Him! Be blessed!

Servants, obey your masters in everything. Obey all the time, even when they can't see you. Don't just pretend to work hard so that they will treat you well. No, you must serve your masters honestly because you respect the Lord. In all the work you are given, do the best you can. Work as though you are working for the Lord, not any earthly master. Remember that you will receive your reward from the Lord, who will give you what he promised his people. Yes, you are serving Christ. He is your real Master.

—Colossians 3:22–24 (ERV)

Remember the saying, "When the cat's away, the mice will play"? This means that what you do when someone is not looking doesn't matter. We know it does matter, but sometimes we like to think it doesn't. But God sees past the outside appearance and into our hearts. No matter how things appear to be in our lives, God knows the appearance of our heart! He wants to be the reason we do what we do and how well we do it, not to earn His favor, but to honor Him and His Son, who died for us. The work was done on the cross by Christ. What we are to do with our gift of life, is to honor that job well done.

Walk with Him! Be blessed!

Sprinkled with the blood of Christ, our hearts have been made free from a guilty conscience, and our bodies have been washed with pure water. So come near to God with a sincere heart, full of confidence because of our faith in Christ. We must hold on to the hope we have, never hesitating to tell people about it. We can trust God to do what he promised.

—Hebrews 10:22–23 (ERV)

Guilt puts the focus on us and on what we have or haven't done. So when we are encouraged to come near to God full of confidence and free from a guilty conscience, it isn't because we have performed well and are confident that God will welcome us with open arms based on our merits. It is because we are covered with the blood of Christ, which was shed on the cross. Therefore, we can approach God with confidence and without guilt, because our faith is in Christ, not in ourselves. When we focus on Christ, our guilt is lifted and we can experience the freedom that Christ bought. That is what we are encouraged to talk about. It is what we shouldn't hesitate to share with others—the hope found in the promises of God.

Walk with Him! Be blessed!

The world of the generous gets larger and larger; the world of the stingy gets smaller and smaller. The one who blesses others is abundantly blessed; those who help others are helped.

—Proverbs 11:24–25 (MSG)

Sounds good, doesn't it? Be generous and your world gets larger and larger. Bless others and you will be blessed abundantly. Help others and you are guaranteed help. But be careful to understand what God means by your world getting larger and larger. It doesn't mean you get more of what you want. It very well might mean that you are given more responsibility to do more for others. (Remember the verse "To those who are given much, much is asked"?) Blessing others might not mean you will be blessed with something you desire. It might very well mean that your blessing is in the blessing of others. Also remember that the help we receive in return for helping may not look like the help we are expecting. Remember that God's ways are not our ways and that His thoughts are not our thoughts.

Walk with Him! Be blessed!

Now you are wearing a new life, a life that is new every day. You are growing in your understanding of the one who made you. You are becoming more and more like him. In this new life it doesn't matter if you are a Greek or a Jew, circumcised or not. It doesn't matter if you speak a different language or even if you are a Scythian. It doesn't matter if you are a slave or free. Christ is all that matters, and he is in all of you.

—Colossians 3:10–11 (ERV)

Diversity has become a widely used word in the last ten years. A lot has been brought to our attention about how diverse our country is and how different we all are. I agree that our country is made up of people from a lot of different backgrounds and cultures, which is one of the many reasons that the United States is the best nation on the entire planet. But when so much focus is put on our differences, we tend to forget how much alike we are and what we have in common. Even in the church (the body of believers), we get caught up in how different one group of believers is from another group.

The verse above encourages us to see and hold onto the One we share, Christ, and to know that He is in all of us. Our differences only matter if they get in the way of what we truly share: our love for Christ. If we allow differences to keep us from seeing what we have in common, then the differences have become a problem. Christ is all that matters to those who believe, and He is in us all. Walk with Him! Be blessed!

That's right because I, your God, have a firm grip on you and I am not letting go. I am telling you don't panic! I am right here to help you!

—Isaiah 41:13 (MSG)

How many times a day should we remind ourselves of this promise in the Word? I believe that I should hear it at least five times an hour. I allow this world to toss me around like a rag doll almost continually. I keep my hand on the panic button, ready to go full throttle into panic mode. Sometimes I think I am more comfortable being panicked than resting in the assurance that my heavenly Father has me and has promised not to let go. Maybe that is my problem. I am more comfortable in panic mode than in the assurance of my Father because I have practiced panic more than assurance. I think I need to change what I am practicing. How about you?

Walk with Him! Be blessed!

God has chosen you and made you his holy people. He loves you. So your new life should be like this: Show mercy to others. Be kind, humble, gentle, and patient. Don't be angry with each other, but forgive each other. If you feel someone has wronged you, forgive them. Forgive others because the Lord forgave you. Together with these things, the most important part of your new life is to love each other. Love is what holds everything together in perfect unity. Let the peace that Christ gives control your thinking. It is for peace that you were chosen to be together in one body. And always be thankful. Let the teaching of Christ live inside you richly. Use all wisdom to teach and counsel each other. Sing psalms, hymns, and spiritual songs with thankfulness in your hearts to God. Everything you say and everything you do should be done for Jesus your Lord. And in all you do, give thanks to God the Father through Jesus.

—Colossians 3:12–17 (ERV)

In the verses above, we are told that we are Christ's holy people and He loves us, yet we tend to think that living holy lives means we won't experience struggles or hardships. We all know that life is filled with hardships, so living holy lives, as these verses tell us to do, seems almost impossible. Being holy doesn't mean we are to be perfect. To be holy means we are purified, just like Christ purified us on the cross. We must become holy, and that happens by being purified, by having unholy things removed from our life. When gold is purified, it is put under extreme heat so all the impurities are burned away. Unfortunately, when the Lord is purifying us and removing the unholy things from our life, we tend to think that He has forsaken us instead of seeing it as His mighty work in our life, bringing us into the relationship He died on the cross for us to have. So maybe we should begin to see *all* things of our lives as part of the process we need to undergo so we can be purified and become holy. The goldsmith knows the gold has become purified when he can see his reflection in the piece he is working on, and that only comes after the piece has been under extreme pressure. Maybe the Lord is just desiring to see Himself in you so that you can live as the verses above say, by being part of His holy people.

Walk with Him! Be blessed!

Many of the Samaritan people in that town believed in Jesus. They believed because of what the woman had told them about him. She had told them, "He told me everything I have ever done." The Samaritans went to Jesus. They begged him to stay with them. So he stayed there two days. Many more people became believers because of the things he said. The people said to the woman, "First we believed in Jesus because of what you told us. But now we believe because we heard him ourselves. We know now that he really is the one who will save the world."

—John 4:39–42 (ERV)

These verses come at the end of the story about the woman at the well. After her conversation with Jesus at the well, the woman went back to her town and witnessed to the people, saying, "I think the Messiah is at the well. Come and see for yourself!" And the people did go and see for themselves. They believed because of the testimony of the woman, which is really cool. We are called to bring people to Christ by sharing the testimony of His presence in our lives. But even cooler is that after the people believed because of the woman's testimony, they spent time with Christ. After just two days they said, "We believed first because of what you [the woman] said, but now we believe because we have heard Him ourselves, and we know He is the Messiah!" They went from believing because of someone else's testimony to having their own testimony. Their faith had become their faith, one no longer based off of someone else's testimony. Does your faith come from hearing someone else's testimony, or have you allowed Jesus to give you your own testimony of Him?

Walk with Him! Be blessed!

When you do good, you stop ignorant people from saying foolish things about you. This is what God wants. Live like free people, but don't use your freedom as an excuse to do evil. Live as those who are serving God. Show respect for all people. Love your brothers and sisters in God's family. Respect God, and honor the king.

—1 Peter 2:15–17 (ERV)

People are going to say what they are going to say, especially in today's world. But the question is, do we give them a reason to say what they say? God wants us not to give people a reason to say what they do say about our faith in Christ. You see, *ignorant* means "uninformed," so if people are uninformed about what we believe, then, yes, they will say foolish things about our beliefs. So how do we inform them? By not taking on the burdens the world offers; living in the freedom that Christ's death brings us; serving God by showing respect for all people; and loving our brothers and sisters in Christ, even those we don't always agree with. Of course people will say foolish things about our faith, especially if we don't teach them what we believe by the way we live.

Walk with Him! Be blessed.

One of the teachers of the law came to Jesus. He heard Jesus arguing with the Sadducees and the Pharisees. He saw that Jesus gave good answers to their questions. So he asked him, "Which of the commands is the most important?" Jesus answered, "The most important command is this: 'People of Israel, listen! The Lord our God is the only Lord. Love the Lord your God with all your heart, all your soul, all your mind, and all your strength.' The second most important command is this: 'Love your neighbor the same as you love yourself.' These two commands are the most important." The man answered, "That was a good answer, Teacher. You are right in saying that God is the only Lord and that there is no other God. And you must love God with all your heart, all your mind, and all your strength. And you must love others the same as you love yourself. These commands are more important than all the animals and sacrifices we offer to God."

—Mark 12:28–33 (ERV)

It is interesting how the man in the verse above asked Jesus which commandment was the most important and then, after Jesus answered him, repeated what Jesus had said, adding, "These commands are more important than all the animal sacrifices we offer to God." If this man knew that loving the Lord with all your heart, mind, and strength, and loving your neighbor as you love yourself, was more pleasing to God than sacrificing animals was, then why did he have such issues with Jesus? Maybe because he was busy trying to please God on his own terms and in his own way that he couldn't recognize God's perfect love standing right in front of him. Just like the man said, it isn't the sacrifice of animals that pleases God; it is returning the love that God has given us through His Son by loving others, and that pleases God.

Walk with Him! Be blessed!

Count it all joy, my brothers, when you meet trials of various kinds, for you know that the testing of your faith produces steadfastness. And let steadfastness have its full effect, that you may be perfect and complete, lacking in nothing.

—James 1:2–4 (ESV)

Each year, we in the United States have an official day of thanks. We take the time with family and friends to give thanks for all the blessings in our lives. We are a blessed nation and have so much to be thankful for, but I want to throw you a curveball. How about we find something we don't see as a blessing and give thanks for it, whatever it may be? Why? Because doing so produces in us steadfastness in our Lord, and through Him we become complete, lacking in nothing. If our trials bring us into closer fellowship with our Savior and heavenly Father, then I say, "Amen. They are well worth it!"

Walk with Him! Be blessed!

We have freedom now, because Christ made us free. So stand strong in that freedom. Don't go back into slavery again.

—Galatians 5:1 (ERV)

On July 4 each year, we United States citizens celebrate the freedom of our great country. July 4 marks the day in our history when many men and woman said, "Enough of living in bondage. We choose freedom and are willing to pay the price for the freedom we believe in!" And what a price was paid, and is still being paid, for the freedom we believe in, which is very important to each individual in our great country and throughout the world. There are two other, even more important days in history when freedom was bought: the day Christ died on the cross and the day He rose to set us free from the bondage of sin. Just like the verse says, individuals who have accepted the freedom of Christ must stand strong in those freedoms or else go back into slavery. The same is true for America. So the next time the holiday rolls around, happy Fourth of July!

Walk with Him! Be blessed!

So through Jesus we should never stop offering our sacrifice to God. That sacrifice is our praise, coming from lips that speak his name. And don't forget to do good and to share what you have with others, because sacrifices like these are very pleasing to God.

—Hebrews 13:15–16 (ERV)

The Old Testament mentions sacrifice after sacrifice offered to God. From what I understand, these sacrifices were offered to atone for the day's, month's, or year's wrongs or to get a new start with God. But after Christ died on the cross and provided the final blood sacrifice for sin, we began our new relationship with God differently, through Christ. We don't require a priest to go into the holiest of holy places to offer sacrifices for us, because Christ is the final priest now sitting at the right hand of God. His offering of His own blood completed the sacrifice of blood to absolve people of their sins. Now we are able to offer the sacrifice of ourselves to God through our praises to Him, by the way we speak of Him, and by the way we care for others. That is, our daily life has become a sacrifice. These are the sacrifices that are pleasing to God. Walk with Him! Be blessed!

Jesus Christ is the same yesterday, today, and forever. Don't let all kinds of strange teachings lead you into the wrong way. Depend only on God's grace for spiritual strength, not on rules about foods. Obeying those rules doesn't help anyone.

—Hebrews 13:8–9 (ERV)

Maybe I was in a bubble growing up, but I thought everyone believed in Jesus, who is celebrated at Christmas and Easter. Maybe I was just a kid and thought as simply as my simple life was. My first realization that others had other beliefs came when I was a teenager and first heard about something called cults. At that time, I thought that a cult was a strange and weird thing. *There are people who don't believe that Jesus is Jesus? Weird!* But as I have seen throughout my life, the message of Jesus is often moved from the front lines of daily life and mixed in with different messages from both inside and outside the church about who Christ is and what He said or what was meant by what He said. It is evident that not everyone believes that Jesus is the Jesus I celebrate at Christmas and Easter. It is those two events—Christ's birth and His resurrection—that define my belief in who He is. Without those events being at the center of my beliefs, then, yes, I could become easily confused with everything the world tries to feed me about Him. But because of those two events, I can depend on God's grace for the spiritual strength and clarity I need to sift through all the strange teachings that bombard me daily. I hope that you, too, find your clarity in the message of the manger and the cross and all the *truth* in between. Walk with Him! Be blessed!

We have all these great people around us as examples. Their lives tell us what faith means. So we, too, should run the race that is before us and never quit. We should remove from our lives anything that would slow us down and the sin that so often makes us fall. We must never stop looking to Jesus. He is the leader of our faith, and he is the one who makes our faith complete. He suffered death on a cross. But he accepted the shame of the cross as if it were nothing because of the joy he could see waiting for him. And now he is sitting at the right side of God's throne. Think about Jesus. He patiently endured the angry insults that sinful people were shouting at him. Think about him so that you won't get discouraged and stop trying.

—Hebrews 12:1–3 (ERV)

Verse 1 reminds us that we have been given many examples of people who can show us what faith is and that we should use their examples to help us run our own race and never give up. We are told to get rid of anything that slows us down (distractions this world offers) or causes us to fall (sin) while running our race. After verse 1 reminds us of the examples we have in people and how those examples can help us to run our race well, verse 2 reminds us that Christ is the One we are to never stop looking to. People may be great examples of Christ, but they are not Christ. Christ is the One who took the shame of the cross. Christ completes of our faith. His Word endures forever. He is seated at the right hand of God. Think about Christ so that you don't get discouraged and give up. Be careful not to let the examples of faith replace the *leader* of your faith. Walk with Him! Be blessed!

I have told you these things so that you can have peace because of me. In this world you will have trouble. But cheer up! I have won the battle over the world.

—John 16:33 (NIRV)

We are not promised a life free from struggles. Actually, we are told that we will have struggles. But we are promised a peace that is unexplainable when we are in Christ, because our trust is in Him and not in this world, and because He has already overcome, and will once again overcome, this world when He returns. Walk with Him! Be blessed!

> Dear brothers and sisters, when troubles of any kind come your way, consider it an opportunity for great joy. For you know that when your faith is tested, your endurance has a chance to grow. So let it grow, for when your endurance is fully developed, you will be perfect and complete, needing nothing.

> —James 1:2–4 (NLT)

When big trouble comes, we try to apply this verse and do a pretty good job of convincing ourselves that it is time for our faith to grow. But what about the little everyday annoyances we face? The checker at the checkout stand is rude; a guy driving a car cuts you off; or your hair just decided to have a really bad day. These little tests of faith are just as important for growing our endurance as the big trials we may have to endure. It is our attitude toward those things that makes the difference.

It is like this: before one can run five miles comfortably, one must first run one mile comfortably. It is mile one, two, three, and four that train us to run that fifth mile. So instead of seeing the daily trials and tests as annoyances, maybe we should be found faithful in the little things so that we can be trusted with the bigger things. No matter the size of our trials, they all help us grow in our faith. With this type of attitude, we will begin to see every moment of our life as being God-designed.

Walk with Him! Be blessed!

Being confident in this, that he who began a good work in you will carry it through to completion until the day of our Lord.

—Philippians 1:6 (NIV)

Even when it seems that the Lord is not working around you, remember that He is working in you. He will never leave you or forsake you! What the Lord has begun, He will finish. Walk with Him! Be blessed!

Peace I leave with you; my peace I give to you. Not as the world gives do I give to you. Let not your hearts be troubled, neither let them be afraid.

—John 14:27 (ESV)

Do not be anxious about anything, but in everything by prayer and supplication with thanksgiving let your requests be made known to God. And the peace of God, which surpasses all understanding, will guard your hearts and your minds in Christ Jesus.

—Philippians 4:6–7 (ESV)

I have said these things to you, that in me you may have peace. In the world you will have tribulation. But take heart; I have overcome the world.

—John 16:33 (ESV)

Peace I leave with you; my peace I give to you. Not as the world gives do I give to you. Let not your heart be troubled, neither let it be afraid.

—John 14:27 (ESV)

I am thinking that God wants us to have peace in our lives. So why don't we? Why are we always struggling to have the peace that is evident and that is available to us from God? Could it be that we don't have the correct understanding of what the peace of God is? Maybe we think peace means the absence of turmoil or conflict, when what is promised is an assurance during difficult times (we will have them!). Or maybe we don't know how to feel close to God unless we are having to search for the peace we actually already have! In this world of constant chaos, maybe we have just become more comfortable searching for the peace of God than actually living in the peace of God.

Don't let the search for peace become what keeps drawing you to Christ when you are already in the presence of Christ. For in His presence is the peace. To know He will never leave us or forsake us in times of chaos or calm ends the search. Christ reminded us of this when He said upon returning to heaven, "My peace I leave with you." Walk with Him! Be blessed!

As for God, his way is perfect: The Lord's word is flawless; he shields all who take refuge in him.

—2 Samuel 22:31 (NIV)

Wow, oh wow: God's way is perfect. He is perfect! Through His flawless Word, He speaks life into our imperfect life. God is our shield from this world if we go to Him while trusting and resting in Him and His promises. Wow, what promises we have from God our heavenly Father! Walk with Him! Be blessed!

Jesus answered, "'Love the Lord your God with all your heart, with all your soul, with all your strength, and with all your mind'; and 'Love your neighbor as you love yourself.'"

—Luke 10:27 (GNT)

Jesus was asked what was the greatest commandment. The people who asked were probably surprised when He said that the greatest is to love the Lord your God with everything you are and then to love your neighbor as you love yourself. That part, "as you love yourself," always makes me think, *Oops!* Jesus tells us how to love God (with everything we have), but then He says, essentially, "Oh, and since you know how to love yourself, love others that way!" We should apply this wisdom to the selfie world we live in. Jesus knew that even today this verse would speak to us, as He knew that we would be lovers of self before lovers of others. But if we tie this verse to the golden rule—"So in everything you do, do to others what you would have them do to you. This sums up the law and the prophets" (Matthew 7:12 NIV)—then we have some instruction on how to live out the second greatest commandment. You know how you want others to treat you, and you know how you want to be loved, so treat and love others in that way. You want to be loved unconditionally, so you love unconditionally. You want to be forgiven when you have done wrong, so you forgive when you have been wronged. You want others to consider their impact on you, so you consider your impact on them. At Kanakuk Kamps (Christian summer camps), it is presented this way: I am third. First comes God, next comes others, and last comes self. I believe that Christ meant this when He said that the greatest commandment is to "love the Lord your God with all your heart, with all your soul, with all your strength, and with all your mind" and to "love your neighbor as you love yourself."

Walk with Him! Be blessed.

A truly good friend will openly correct you. You can trust a friend who corrects you, but kisses from an enemy are nothing but lies.

—Proverbs 27:5–6 (CEV)

"You can't handle the truth" (name the movie this comes from) is a statement that typifies the world we live in. We are asked to sugarcoat or adjust what we say so as not to offend someone. I do agree that we all need to filter out words because there are too many verbal offenses being shared, but when it comes to personal relationships, we are called to be honest with our friends and family (or they need to be honest with us) even if they (or we) don't want to hear it. Example: toward the end of one school year, one of my favorite classes (fourteen high school boys and four high school girls) were getting a lot more active than usual, so I had to corral them a little more than I'd done previously. One day one of my students said, "Miss, do you not like us anymore?"

I replied, "Why do you ask that?"

He said, "You are always getting on us!"

My response was, "It is because I like you that I discipline you! I want the best for you. If something is getting in the way of your getting the most out of this class, then I need to do my best to get you to remove it! And if that requires disciplining you, then I must discipline you!"

Wow. How many times do you think Christ says that to us when people are (or Christ is) being honest with us about something we take offense to or when we think as the world tells us and we believe that people don't (or Jesus doesn't) love us anymore? We need to realize it is because of people's love for us that they are honest with us or send discipline our way. The honesty of Christ or a kiss from the Enemy: which one do you choose?

Walk with Him! Be blessed!

My son do not forget my teachings but keep my commands in your hearts!

—Proverbs 3:1 (NIV)

How can you remember something you never knew? It used to be that people knew what was in the Bible, whether they knew the whole Bible or not. The Word of God used to be woven into people's daily lives, and most everyone attended some type of church service at least once a week. What I am trying to say is this: our God gave us His Word to reveal Himself to us. How can we get to know Him who created us if we don't spend time getting to know Him through the ways He has created for us, namely, church, the Bible, prayer, fellowship with other believers, and Christian songs? How can we hide something in our hearts like He asked us to do if we don't know what to hide?

Walk with Him! Be blessed!

Keep your lives free from the love of money, and be satisfied with what you have. For God has said, "I will never leave you; I will never abandon you."

—Hebrews 13:5 (GNT)

"For I know the plans I have for you," declares the Lord, "plans to prosper you and not to harm you, plans to give you hope and a future."

—Jeremiah 29:11 (NIV)

Jesus Christ is the same yesterday, today, and forever.

—Hebrews 13:8 (GNT)

If someone were to ask you to enter into a relationship with him or her and then made just these three promises—(1) I will never abandon you, never! (2) I have a great plan for you, and it is for you never to lose hope. I guarantee you a future that has already been taken care of. (3) I promise to always be the same. No matter how you come to me, I will always be open-armed and loving toward you! There is nothing you could do that will change who I am. I never change!—would you jump in and not look back, or would you be skeptical because of the revolving-door relationships we have come to expect in our lives? Not many people would or could make these types of promises and keep them, but these promises weren't made by a person. They were made by the Creator, God Almighty, and His Son, the One who willingly died on the cross for you and me! Unfortunately too many times when we read the promises given to us by God in His Word, we respond as if they are coming from just another person, not from our Lord and Savior. It is because of our response that we question if these promises can really be trusted. We need to let go of our human perspective of God and Christ so we can begin to know Him as who He is: God! Because God can make these promises because He knows He will keep them. If you read His Word, then you will find that these are just three of the numerous promises from Him who created us and who sent His Son to live, die, and rise from the dead for us—promises that can be easily trusted when we truly realize from where they come. Walk with Him! Be blessed!

Let them give thanks to the Lord for his unfailing love and his wonderful deeds for mankind, for he satisfies the thirsty and fills the hungry with good things.

—Psalms 107:8–9 (NIV)

Give thanks to God, who knows and provides for all our needs even before we know we have them. From the beginning of time (which God created), He knew we would need a Savior. Through His perfect plan of Christ's being born, dying on the cross, and being resurrected, that need has been met! To Him be the glory, praise, and thanks. Walk with Him! Be blessed!

> Paul gathered up a bundle of sticks and was putting them on the fire when a snake came out on account of the heat and fastened itself to his hand. The natives saw the snake hanging on Paul's hand and said to one another, "This man must be a murderer, but Fate will not let him live, even though he escaped from the sea." But Paul shook the snake off into the fire without being harmed at all. They were waiting for him to swell up or suddenly fall down dead. But after waiting for a long time and not seeing anything unusual happening to him, they changed their minds and said, "He is a god!"

—Acts 28:3–6 (GNT)

It is a good thing that Paul understood who he was in Christ and didn't let the opinions of others affect him. In the opinions of those around him, Paul went from "he must be a murderer" to "he must be a god!" This happened within a matter of minutes, all because the people were looking at the events happening to Paul to determine who he was. They couldn't see how God was working in Paul's life.

There are two lessons here: (1) If we let the opinions of others, not Christ, determine who we are, then we will continually be tossed back and forth like the boat Paul was on until one day, just like the boat, we will be damaged so badly that we will no longer stay afloat. (2) If we look at someone else and try to determine what is going on in his or her life (or why it is going on), we can totally miss God's work in their life all together!

God had been preparing Paul for this journey, the shipwreck, and even the snakebite. Taken together, these things looked like a bad situation, but they were all a part of God's plan. Within a few days of being on the island, Paul had healed a man with a high fever and many others who had come to him. After staying there for three months, he sailed to another island and then went on to Rome, where Paul's testimony of Christ brought others to Him. God had a plan for Paul even if others couldn't see it because they were looking at the events around him and not for God's involvement in his life.

Walk with Him! Be blessed!

Jesus Christ is the same yesterday today and forever!

—Hebrews 13:8 (NIV)

In this world where many things are subject to constant change, we should turn to the One who remains the same. The life He lived and the words He spoke over two thousand years ago still have the same meaning and bring the same comfort. He is your Rock and your fortress! Walk with Him! Be blessed!

> So Ananias went and found Saul. He laid his hands on him and said, "Brother Saul, the Lord Jesus, who appeared to you on the road, has sent me so that you might regain your sight and be filled with the Holy Spirit." Instantly something like scales fell from Saul's eyes, and he regained his sight. Then he got up and was baptized.

—Acts 9:17–18 (NLT)

Many of us are like Saul in that it takes an encounter with Christ for us to begin to realize how blind we have been while walking through life. After we read about how Ananias came to Saul and see that the scales were removed from Saul's eyes, we begin to get the symbolism: not only was Saul (who later took the name Paul) physically blind for three days, but also he was spiritually blind for many years before that.

Throughout his ministry, Paul talked about his life before his encounter with Christ on the road to Damascus. Previously, he found his righteousness in who he was. About his lineage and his heritage he said, "In this I boasted!" But after Christ called him out for persecuting Him and Saul was blinded, Saul began to "see clearly," first who Christ is and second who he himself was—a sinner in need of a Savior.

Many of us are still blinded by the things of this world, which we have bought into in order to validate ourselves. Many of us are farsighted, thinking, *Oh, someday I will let go of this, but for now it is okay if I still keep it in my line of vision.* Some are nearsighted, seeing all the things in their life that look like parts of a Christian life yet, like Saul, looking at the things of this world to bring them into a relationship with Him. Not until the scales over our eyes are removed can we, just like Paul, come to see, and come to know how blinded we have been while walking through life. Only then, with the clear vision that comes from seeing who Christ is and who we are, "a sinner in need of a Savior," do we begin to see ourselves and others with the same sight Christ sees with. Walk with Him! Be blessed!

Yes, what joy for those whose record the Lord has cleared of guilt, whose lives are lived in complete honesty!

—Psalms 32:2 (NLT)

Honesty is an interesting thing, but it is almost a forgotten thing in the world today. Honesty has been replaced with justification, but not the kind we receive from Christ. This justification is the kind that allows us to be okay with our guilt because we are justified in our actions, when our actions clearly go against what we are called to do as followers of Christ. We tend to justify ourselves or other people in many different ways, such as, "He is really a good kid, but he comes from such a rough and difficult family. There is a lot going on at home right now" (I hear this a lot about kids) or "It doesn't really matter, because my actions only affect me. My choice is my choice" (even if it is a bad choice, it does affect others!). Another person might say, "I just said it. I wasn't really thinking. Oops, my bad!" When we say these sorts of things, all we are doing is covering up the guilt, which keeps us from being honest with others, ourselves, and most importantly our Savior.

Measuring our "my bad" moments from the world's perspective doesn't allow us to be completely honest with whom we need to be honest with most: Christ. We need Him to clear our record, which He did on the cross for eternity, but we also need Him daily so we can walk honestly with Him in newness of life and in the true justification He gives. Walk with Him! Be blessed!

I [the Lord] will instruct you and teach you in the way you should go; I will counsel you with My eye upon you.

—Psalms 32:8 (AB)

How amazing: the Lord instructs us along our way. Being a teacher, I definitely understand instruction. I know that when I instruct, I usually have a definite direction in mind toward which I am leading the instruction. In the teaching profession, this is called a lesson plan. Lesson plans give the instructor a path to travel in order to guide the student(s). Now, after many years of teaching many different students, the one thing I as an instructor have come to know is this: Whatever the main objective of the lesson, every student goes down the path differently! Some run, some skip, some lag, some stumble, and some just flat-out fall. Some stop along the way, getting distracted by things that aren't on the path they are being encouraged to walk. Some run off the path and never get back on. No matter how different each student behaves on the path, the objective is still the same: to come to know what is in the plan. Christ has a plan for each of us, to come to the Father through Him. He promises to instruct us in His plan no matter how we go down the path.

Walk with Him! Be blessed!

"Live your life in a manner that others will want what you have." I have heard this said a lot as a message, especially as a youth group message. Goodness, I have said it a lot myself when speaking to people, especially young people. I totally get what the message is meant to encourage. I know what I meant when I said it, but how it might have been heard is another thing. Lately when I have heard this said, it has caused me to grimace. Here is why: we live in a world that encourages us to live in a manner that makes others want to be us. When others envy you, your life, or your stuff, then you have arrived! Now I know that isn't what anyone who delivers the above message means. I know it definitely wasn't what I meant when I encouraged other people, including my daughters, to live in such a way that would make others want what they have. I meant, "Live in such a way that others want Jesus in their life. Make it about Jesus, not about you and your life." And since this world comes at us with so many confusing messages, we should make sure our message is plain, simple, and straightforward: "Live your life so that others desire Jesus!" Since Jesus is what we have, Jesus is what others should want. As it says in Galatians 5:26 (NIV), "Let us not become conceited, provoking one another, envying one another." Besides, others shouldn't really want what we have, as they will have their own personal relationship with Christ, which is exactly what is available for them, because, well, Christ is just that glorious.

Walk with Him! Be blessed!

"For I know the plans I have for you," declares the Lord, "plans to prosper you and not to harm you, plans to give you hope and a future."

—Jeremiah 29:11 (NIV)

This verse is in great use during the time of high school and college graduations, and during the spring wedding season. It is very appropriate and comforting for us when we are going through life changes, even the ones we have looked forward to. But the verse shouldn't be overlooked when seeking something to apply to our normal, everyday life. Our heavenly Father loves us so much that there isn't a part of our life He is overlooking. From the big events to the everyday events, He has a plan to love and care for us, whether we call out to Him or not. He knows the plans He has for us, plans to prosper us and not harm us, plans for a hope-filled future. Remember that daily He has a plan for us. Walk with Him! Be blessed!

My dear friends, you should be quick to listen and slow to speak or to get angry. If you are angry, you cannot do any of the good things God wants done.

—James 1:19–20 (CEV)

We live in such a cluttered world that it is easy to see a contrast to this verse. We are quick to speak and slow to listen, often looking for a fight.

Have you ever considered how this verse applies to prayer? Many times we go to the Lord ready to speak our words of want, desire, and need, yet we don't slow down enough to hear Him reply, to listen to Him speak. And then we get angry, frustrated, and upset when we think that God has not listened to our prayers, requests, and desires. We begin to doubt His ways and His promises because we don't get a response to *all* of the requests we have put to Him. Maybe if we came to Him as these verses say, quick to listen, and slow to speak or become angry, then we would begin to hear Him. And then we would begin to be able to do all the good things God wants done.

Walk with Him! Be blessed!

You bless them by saying, "You told me your sins, without trying to hide them, and now I forgive you." Before I confessed my sins, my bones felt limp, and I groaned all day long. Night and day your hand weighed heavily on me, and my strength was gone as in the summer heat. So I confessed my sins and told them all to you. I said, "I'll tell the Lord each one of my sins." Then you forgave me and took away my guilt.

—Psalms 32:2–5 (CEV)

Coming clean before God is good for the soul. The ironic thing is that God already knows our iniquities. When we confess them, it isn't to inform Him, as if we know something He doesn't know. Rather, it is to be honest with Him and acknowledge our need for Him. Trying to deny that need by not confessing our sin causes illness, not just physical illness but also illness in our soul. The guilt weighs us down, and we just don't do well under the burden of guilt. When we confess our need for Christ in our life, the burden of guilt is removed and we can walk in the freedom gained by Christ's death and resurrection. Walk with Him! Be blessed!

Peace I leave with you; my peace I give to you. Not as the world gives do I give to you. Let not your hearts be troubled, neither let them be afraid.

—John 14:27 (ESV)

These words are ones that Jesus spoke before He ascended to heaven. If you look up the definition of *peace* in a dictionary, you will find that it means "freedom from war or strife." But this cannot be what Christ meant when He said, "Peace I leave with you!" He went on to explain, "Not peace like the world gives." So what did He mean when mentioning peace? Well, maybe that can be explained by some other verses He gave us. "I have said these things to you, that in me you may have peace. In the world you will have tribulation. But take heart; I have overcome the world" (John 16:33 ESV) promises us that we will have trials but encourages us not to lose heart, to continue in the peace we have already received from Him. Romans 8:6 reads, "The mind set on flesh is death but the mind set on the spirit is life and peace." In Romans 14:17–19 (ESV) we are told, "For the kingdom of God is not a matter of eating and drinking but of righteousness and peace and joy in the Holy Spirit. Whoever thus serves Christ is acceptable to God and approved by men. So then let us pursue what makes for peace and for mutual up building." Once again we are encouraged to let peace be our guide. So when trials come, you should walk in the peace you have already received from your relationship with Christ. Then you will know that peace is not the absence of wars and strife but is what we have during such times because of what Christ did on the cross.

Walk with Him! Be blessed!

And Jesus grew in wisdom and stature, and in favor with God and man.

—Luke 2:52 (NIV)

May we all be like Christ and grow in wisdom (the godly kind), stature (may we take care of our physical body, as it is the only one we have), and favor (may we be the kind of person people like to see coming their way). May we be more of a giver than a taker with humankind and, more importantly, with God.

Walk with Him! Be blessed!

The Lord your God is in your midst, a mighty one who will save; he will rejoice over you with gladness; he will quiet you by his love; he will exult over you with loud singing.

—Zephaniah 3:17 (ESV)

It seems sometimes that the verses that jump off the pages of God's Word are the ones that talk about quiet, rest, and peace. This one reminds me that the Lord is in our midst. Water vapor is everywhere in the form of mist even if we don't feel it or see it. It is in the atmosphere just like the Lord our God, who is wherever we are. (Yes, I took the liberty of replacing *midst* with *mist*. Work with me here.) The next thing we are told is that He saves. He saves us for eternity, but do we consider during our roughest days that there is still more that we are saved from in the crazy world because the presence of our God is where we are? And while there, He is rejoicing over us. Do I really give Him reason to rejoice? Probably not, but in spite of me He is rejoicing with gladness just because I am His, no matter how unworthily I present myself to Him. In all of the madness of life, it is because of His love that I can walk in peace and quiet—only because of His presence.

Now for the most interesting part of this verse (for me, anyway): He is singing loudly over me. Really? Why don't I hear it if the God of the universe is singing loudly? Maybe it is because I am allowing everything else to be much louder in my life. God's voice can and will be heard if I turn down all the other things I keep turning up the volume for. When I turn down the volume of those other things, I will hear His quiet but loud voice singing and rejoicing over me, reminding me that He is present wherever I choose to go.

Choose your steps wisely today. Walk with Him! Be blessed!

"For my thoughts are not your thoughts, neither are your ways my ways," declares the Lord.

—Isaiah 55:8 (NIV)

We seem not to realize that we are not God. We did not create this thing called life; He did! He created us to have a relationship with Him through His Son, Jesus. We never will get everything figured out, and what we do get figured out only stays that way for a moment before it changes. That is unsettling to a lot of people, believers in Christ and nonbelievers alike. We all just want to know and understand this thing called life. Well, the longer I live, the more I give up my ways for God's ways without having to understand or control my life.

This verse brings me such peace. He who designed me has promised to fix me. (He still has a lot of fixing to do in me. Praise to the Lord, who is so very patient.) My thoughts don't even come close to His thoughts. If I don't get out of His arms, then He will carry me through this day, whether I understand His ways or not.

Walk with Him! Be blessed!

But as for me, I will pray to you, Lord; answer me, God at a time you choose. Answer me because of your great love, because you keep your promise to save.

—Psalms 69:13 (GNT)

It would be amazing if we prayed this prayer and really meant it when we felt the need to ask God for direction, wisdom, or something we needed. Imagine really meaning it when you say, "In Your time, Lord, from Your overly abundant love and from Your saving grace, answer this prayer." Instead, most the time we pray to get our way in our time so that we can do our own thing with God's answer. When I am truly honest with myself, I see that this is the motive behind my prayers. "Answer me, Lord, in my way and in my time, and let me do with Your response as I see fit." O for a heart that truly says, "Lord, take this prayer and, in Your perfect time, from Your perfect, abundant love, and by Your amazing grace, answer me. Whatever Your response may be, please let me be thankful for it. And let me rest knowing that Your answer is better than anything I could ever imagine, even if it is something I do not want." To be truly willing to do God's will for my life, I have come to learn, means that I need to be completely humbled by His presence. To have prayers answered means to be in His presence, which means I must be humbled no matter how He answers me.

Walk with Him! Be blessed!

For I know the thoughts and plans that I have for you, says the Lord, thoughts and plans for welfare and peace and not for evil, to give you hope and a future.

—Jeremiah 29:11 (AB)

This is a great go-to verse when life throws us curveballs and we have no clue what tomorrow will bring (like we ever really do). So we repeat this verse and share it with friends who are unsure of decisions they have to make. All the while we are deciding what God's plans for us are to look like. We all have a little or a lot of Sarah and Abraham in us. God promises us that He has a plan and a promise for our lives. When it doesn't materialize as fast as we would like, we decide to give ourselves a Hagar (read the story of Abraham and Sarah in Genesis 18), something that we think will help speed God's promises along.

God doesn't need our help. He desires us to have faith, to trust in Him, and to have patience for His will to be done so that His glory will be revealed to us and, more importantly, to others. "Do not be anxious for anything, but in every situation by prayer and petition with thanksgiving present your request to the Lord and the peace that surpasses all understanding will guard your heart and your mind" (Philippians 4:6–7 NIV). Patience and peace will sustain us until God opens the door we are waiting on. Until it is opened, we should praise Him who is preparing what is on the other side.

Walk with Him! Be blessed!

Ye are the light of the world. A city set on a hill cannot be hid. Neither do men light a lamp, and put it under the bushel, but on the stand; and it shineth unto all that are in the house.

—Matthew 5:14–15 (ASV)

Do not underestimate your ability to make a difference in this world for Christ. Even if it seems as if your light is dimmed because of the happenings of life, you are still a light in the darkness of this world by being a child of God, by having hope when things appear hopeless, by having faith when things don't turn around instantly, and by praising God when there appears to be no reason (that is, when things aren't easy). We are not promised a life of ease because of our relationship with Christ, but we are promised that we will never be alone, forsaken, or forgotten. It is not how life is, easy or hard, that makes us a light for others. It is our allowing others to see Christ in how we live in this world that makes the difference, remembering that Christ is the Light. Just by opening our hearts to Him, we allow His light to shine through—and the world will see that light in the darkness.

Walk with Him! Be blessed!

God isn't a God of disorder but of peace. Like in all the churches of God's people.

—1 Corinthians 14:33 (CEB)

The earth is spinning at an incredible rate of speed. It does this to keep us in the perfect position in the universe for sustaining life—not too close to the sun and not too far away from the sun. That is amazing to me. And it comforts me to know that God knows exactly how to keep us in this crazy, hectic, out-of-control world: by giving us His Son, to whom we can draw near when our world seems to be spinning out of control. We will be found in the perfect place, at His feet, while praising Him and giving Him thanks and adoration for His sacrifice on the cross for us.

Walk with Him! Be blessed!

Instead, be kind and tender-hearted to one another, and forgive one another, as God has forgiven you through Christ.

—Ephesians 4:32 (GNT)

To forgive someone when he or she has really hurt you is one of the hardest things to do. Unfortunately a lot of the time we feel justified in holding onto the hurt and not forgiving the person. We do this so that the person who harmed us can receive the hurt he or she placed on us by knowing that he or she isn't forgiven. Wow! Realize what that says back to us. When we have someone to forgive in our lives and we refuse to forgive that person, how can we walk in the forgiveness that Christ died to give us? Forgiving someone who has harmed you is more about being free to receive the forgiveness Christ has for you than about just forgiving the person for his or her own sake. We receive freedom as well when we forgive.

Walk with Him! Be blessed!

The Son of Man came to find lost people and save them.

—Luke 19:10 (ERV)

This verse definitely gives hope to the people who have not come to the saving grace of Christ. It also speaks to them about the reason Christ came to live here on earth, so that all who come to Him and believe in Him shall have eternal life. "For God so loved the world He gave His only begotten Son that who so ever believes in Him shall not perish but have eternal life" (John 3:16 KJV). But even if you already have a relationship with Christ, the above verse can speak to you. When you are struggling and feel lost, not knowing which way to turn, know that Jesus is seeking you out and wants to save you from your troubles. This doesn't necessarily mean that your troubles will be removed, but it does mean that He wants to be your hope through them. Just like Jesus is our assurance for eternity, He is our assurance for today. Walk with Him! Be blessed!

For a day in your courts is better than a thousand elsewhere. I would rather be a doorkeeper in the house of my God than dwell in the tents of wickedness.

—Psalms 84:10 (ESV)

Man, this world makes people think it has a lot to offer. But compared to God, does it really? I mean, as soon as you have the world's best, it comes out with something "better." You get your house, clothes, or car in the latest style, and then the world changes what is in. On the other hand, what God offers us is the same yesterday, today, and forever (Hebrews 13:8), which is His Son, Jesus Christ, the Alpha and the Omega (the Beginning and the End). What He spoke at the beginning of creation, He still speaks—and in the same way—today. "In the beginning was the Word and the Word was with God and the Word was God" (John 1:1 NIV). The Word is Christ! What was purposed for humanity at the beginning of time is still purposed for humankind today: an eternal relationship with God through His Son. I don't know about you, but I am going with the One from whom I know what I will get, the One who doesn't change things up on me. Walk with Him! Be blessed!

When the Lord had finished talking with them, he was taken up into heaven and sat down in the place of honor at God's right hand.

—Luke 16:19 (NLT)

There is a misconception that if one is a Christian, one is supposed to be perfect and have a life that is trouble-free. It is the perfection of Christ, not our own perfection, that we receive when we accept Him as our Savior. His perfection allows us to come to God head up without the shame and guilt we once had, not because we are perfect but because He is perfect and sits at the right hand of God and says, "Yes, Father, this is one I died for!"

Walk with Him! Be blessed!

Love is patient and kind; love does not envy or boast; it is not arrogant or rude. It does not insist on its own way; it is not irritable or resentful; it does not rejoice at wrongdoing, but rejoices with the truth. Love bears all things, believes all things, hopes all things, endures all things. Love never ends. As for prophecies, they will pass away; as for tongues, they will cease; as for knowledge, it will pass away. For we know in part and we prophesy in part, but when the perfect comes, the partial will pass away. When I was a child, I spoke like a child, I thought like a child, I reasoned like a child. When I became a man, I gave up childish ways. For now we see in a mirror dimly, but then face to face. Now I know in part; then I shall know fully, even as I have been fully known. So now faith, hope, and love abide, these three; but the greatest of these is love.

—1 Corinthians 13:4–13 (ESV)

We may not understand everything. Our knowledge, wisdom, and insight are limited, but we can love wholeheartedly. We are instructed to love the Lord our God with our whole heart, and then to love our neighbor as we love ourselves. Even without understanding how to do it, we can do it. Why? Because Christ told us that these are the two greatest commandments, to love Him and then to love others. Walk with Him! Be blessed!

Therefore I tell you, do not be anxious about your life, what you will eat or what you will drink, nor about your body, what you will put on. Is not life more than food, and the body more than clothing? Look at the birds of the air: they neither sow nor reap nor gather into barns, and yet your heavenly Father feeds them. Are you not of more value than they? And which of you by being anxious can add a single hour to his span of life? And why are you anxious about clothing? Consider the lilies of the field, how they grow: they neither toil nor spin, yet I tell you, even Solomon in all his glory was not arrayed like one of these. But if God so clothes the grass of the field, which today is alive and tomorrow is thrown into the oven, will he not much more clothe you, O you of little faith? Therefore do not be anxious, saying, "What shall we eat?" or "What shall we drink?" or "What shall we wear?" For the Gentiles seek after all these things, and your heavenly Father knows that you need them all. But seek first the kingdom of God and his righteousness, and all these things will be added to you. Therefore do not be anxious about tomorrow, for tomorrow will be anxious for itself. Sufficient for the day is its own trouble.

—Matthew 6:25–34 (ESV)

God has you today, no matter what the world tells you. You are ever present on His mind. We are instructed to seek Him first before anything. When we do this, we find that He is already with us, has gone before us, and has covered us all over in His love and presence. *Seek* just means "realize." He is with you. Walk with Him! Be blessed!

Show me your ways, Lord, teach me your paths. Guide me in your truth and teach me, for you are God my Savior, and my hope is in you all day long.

—Psalms 25:4–5 (NIV)

I sent up a prayer this morning, hoping that what is described in the verse above is what your heart desires. I prayed that not just today but daily you will truly desire to know God's ways, His path, and His teachings so that your hope is in Him. Walk with Him! Be blessed!

What, then, shall we say in response to these things? If God is for us, who can be against us? He who did not spare his own Son, but gave him up for us all—how will he not also, along with him, graciously give us all things?

—Romans 8:31–32 (NIV)

If you truly grasp that it is God, not this world, that is for you, then the peace that surpasses all understanding will guide your life. You will walk in confidence with your heart bent toward Him who sent His Son to die for you and not toward this world that wants to chew you up and spit you out. You will have confidence in knowing that even though the world may be doing something to you, your heavenly Father is doing something in you and for you. Walk with Him! Be blessed!

For I know the plans I have for you, declares the Lord, plans for welfare and not for evil, to give you a future and a hope. Then you will call upon me and come and pray to me, and I will hear you. You will seek me and find me, when you seek me with all your heart. I will be found by you, declares the Lord, and I will restore your fortunes and gather you from all the nations and all the places where I have driven you, declares the Lord, and I will bring you back to the place from which I sent you into exile.

—Jeremiah 29:11–14 (ESV)

The above is one of the many verses of hope that appear in the Bible. It is interesting how we tend to use it. When money is tight, a job is lost, or a sickness comes and we are not sure how we will make ends meet, we go to the verse that talks about being prospered, right? But this verse means so much more. God knows all our physical needs. He created us. Who else knows the creation better than the Creator does? More importantly, He knows our emotional needs. He knows He created us for a relationship with Him through His Son, who died on the cross so we could not only spend eternity with Him but also walk moment by moment with Him. He came to give life and give it more abundantly, not just through physical comfort but by comforting our souls so that we know we are walking with Him.

Be blessed!

Follow God's example, therefore, as dearly loved children and walk in the way of love, just as Christ loved us and gave himself up for us as a fragrant offering and sacrifice to God.

—Ephesians 5:1–2 (NIV)

We work hard at trying to figure out how to serve God, and over and over He tells us to love as He has loved. Kanakuk Kamp teaches it this way (as I've mentioned before): I am third. God is first, others are second, and self is third. (Kanakuk Kamp is a Christian sports camp. If you haven't heard of it, you should check it out. Note that this is not a paid advertisement, ha-ha! I love that place.) Christ's love for us took Him to the cross. His love for us kept Him there. His love for us placed Him in the tomb. His Father's love for Christ and for us brought Jesus out of that grave. Wow, that is truly love.

Walk with Him! Be blessed!

I can do all this through him who gives me strength.

—Philippians 4:13 (NIV)

In athletics, one of the most quoted Scriptures is the one above. With no disrespect, I call this the genie verse. We have turned it into the go-to verse when we want to make a play, make the winning shot in order to be the hero, or do something we have not prepared to do (e.g., pass a test we didn't study for—oops!). We use this verse in this way for many immediate requests of things we want or need. When Paul said this, it was after he had said, "I have had it all; I have lost it all. I have been the most blessed; I have been the most scorned and through it all I have come to know: I can do all this through him who gives me strength" (Philippians 4:13 NIV). Further down in the chapter, verse 19 reads, "And my God will meet all your needs according to the riches of his glory in Christ Jesus," which almost seems like it should appear before verse 13 because it explains how we can live life through Christ: by knowing that our God has already met our needs.

Whatever today brings, know that you have what you need in order to do what you need to do through Christ, all for His glory. Walk with Him! Be blessed!

Show me the right path O Lord point out the road for me to follow.

—Psalms 25:4 (NIV)

I have to ask myself, *Is that really my prayer, or do I just want God to grant me my every wish and let my life be what I want it to be? Or do I really want to be on His path, His road, where I will truly be following Him?* To do the will of God, I know I need a willing heart, one that is willing to step where He tells me to step, to move when He tells me to move, or to wait when He tells me to wait. To have that kind of heart, I know I must be willing to let go of the things of this world that are interfering with His creating that kind of heart in me.

God does not force His will on us. He wants us to desire Him, and to desire the relationship provided to us by His Son's death on the cross, of our own free will (which He created in us). Will He show me the path where I should walk? Will He point me to the right road? Absolutely! That is not really the question. The real question is, how willing am I to follow Him?

Walk with Him! Be blessed!

Yet the Lord longs to be gracious to you; therefore he will rise up to show you compassion. For the Lord is a God of justice. Blessed are all who wait for him!

—Isaiah 30:18 (NIV)

If you notice, this verse starts with the word *yet*, which indicates that something happened before this was said. In verse 15, the rebellious people are told to wait. In verses 16–17, the rebellious people have moved. The crazy thing is that there was only one person from whom they fled. Even with their disobedience, and in spite of the fact that God instructed them to wait and they did just the opposite of what He asked, God held true to His promise of mercy, grace, and compassion. Verse 18 reads, "Blessed are those who wait on the Lord." In spite of that, God longs to be gracious and compassionate toward us. How many times do we run from what God has for us because we are unwilling to wait on His perfect timing? Probably way too many times. I pray for you today that if the Lord is asking you to just wait, then you will wait. Meanwhile, walk with Him and be blessed!

For the wages of sin is death, but the gift of God is eternal life in Christ Jesus our Lord.

—Romans 6:23 (NIV)

In this world full of people with an entitlement mind-set, every day is a struggle not to live with an attitude of thinking I deserve more than what I have (and to obtain it with little or no effort on my part). But praise be to God for not giving me what I deserve. Because of my sin, I deserve death. It says so right there in Romans 6:23. But because of Christ's free gift, I won't get what I deserve, which is eternal separation from my Creator, my heavenly Father, my Lord, my Savior. I will give thanks and praise today not for getting what I deserve but for not getting what I deserve. The Lord is very good! Walk with Him! Be blessed!

You are my refuge and my shield; I have put my hope in your word. ... Make your face shine on your servant and teach me your decrees. ... May my lips overflow with praise, for you teach me your decrees. ... Let me live that I may praise you, and may your laws sustain me.

—Psalms 119:114, 135, 171, 175 (NIV)

In Psalms 119, the writer is all over the place. Check out the verses in between the ones above and you will see what I mean. In one verse, the writer is declaring how righteous God is, how pure and just God's instructions are, how he knows they are so much better than what this world offers. But then, in his very next breath, the writer seems to feel the need to remind God how corrupt this world is, how he longs to do all that God has asked him to do, and how hard the world makes it to do so, since the writer feels as if he is constantly bombarded with the things and people of this world. He is back and forth, back and forth, all through Psalm 119. But he keeps coming back to, "You are right, God. You are just, God. You sustain me, God!" He knows his only real hope is in God the Father.

I am a lot like the writer of Psalms 119. I am all over the place when it comes to trusting God. The wonderful thing is that in my heart I know He has me. I just need to let go and let God have all of the fears and emotions that this world constantly reminds me I have. My hope for you is that you, too, know He has you—all of you. Rest in Him today as you walk with Him. Be blessed!

Fix these words of mine in your hearts and minds; tie them as symbols on your hands and bind them on your foreheads. Teach them to your children, talking about them when you sit at home and when you walk along the road, when you lie down and when you get up. Write them on the doorframes of your houses and on your gates, so that your days and the days of your children may be many in the land the Lord swore to give your ancestors, as many as the days that the heavens are above the earth.

—Deuteronomy 11:18–21 (NIV)

The verse above pretty much covers every area of our lives that God wants His Word to be a part of and everything we are to be teaching our children about Him when we lie down, when we get up, when we sit, and when we walk. Maybe what is meant by this verse is that we are to live the Word of God for our children. Speaking it is one thing, but for them to see us live it is even better. Walk with Him! Be blessed!

Today is not perfect, but the Lord we serve is. Be thankful, and remember, "Do all things without grumbling and fault finding and complaining [against God] and questioning and doubting [among yourselves]" (Philippians 2:14 AB). We all want the perfect life, don't we, one where it would be easy not to grumble and complain? But as this verse tells us, there is no perfect day, which would indicate that there is no perfect life since life is made up of days. Instead of focusing on our life being perfect, which would make us think the days would be perfect, we should focus on the One who is perfect: our Lord. If we did this, then our grumbling and complaining would be replaced with praise and thankfulness, which in turn would make us be more content with our imperfect days, that is, our life.

Walk with Him! Be blessed!

Humble yourselves, therefore, under God's mighty hand, that he may lift you up in due time. Cast all your anxiety on him because he cares for you.

—1 Peter 5:6–7 (NIV)

Each year in December, we Christians have a celebration of the most blessed event in history, the birth of our Savior, which should make for the most joyous and peace-filled time of the year. But because Christmas has been turned into a buying time of year and has been made all about gifts, we tend to miss out on the gift that was given and what the celebration truly is about. Add to that the general craziness of the world, which each year seems to bring along with it the fear that accompanies the craziness as we go through the celebration of our Christ and end up further from the peace it is supposed to bring and closer to the chaos this world offers. I encourage you to rest in the Lord. Whether we are supposed to be celebrating the reason for the season or a day in July, let the Lord be your peace, comfort, and joy. Walk with Him! Be blessed!

Also, the Spirit helps us. We are very weak, but the Spirit helps us with our weakness. We don't know how to pray as we should, but the Spirit himself speaks to God for us. He begs God for us, speaking to him with feelings too deep for words.

—Romans 8:26 (ERV)

Too many times I just don't know how to pray. So much is on my heart that I can't get anything off it. During these times, my prayers are like, "Here's this, and here's that, and—oh yeah—here is this other thing, Lord. I lift this person up to you, I give you this, and I give you that." I ramble on and on, repeating myself, I am sure.

I am sure God would love to just interrupt me and say, "I got it!"

This verse comforts me very much. It reassures me that I don't have to worry about leaving something off my prayer list. It encourages me to think that I can spend my time in prayer, praising and thanking God, because the Holy Spirit who lives inside of me can and does know what and how to come to the Father for me. I can praise Jesus and let the Holy Spirit do my talking.

Walk with Him! Be blessed!

Even so let your light shine before men; that they may see your good works, and glorify your Father who is in heaven.

—Matthew 5:16 (ASV)

I totally agree with the assertion "You might be the only Jesus someone ever sees" (even though I am not fond of it), but I must be very careful not to read it as, "I might be the only Jesus someone ever sees." When desiring to minister to this sad, hurting, and corrupt world, we must be careful not to let our desire and efforts to fix a problem overshadow God's love. Our works, acts of kindness, and care for others is meaningless if it is not done out of our own personal love for Christ. What others need to see from us is our own personal love for Christ, our own personal faith in Christ, our own personal hope in Christ. I believe that is what is meant by, "You might be the only Jesus someone sees." Christ lived a life of faith, hope, and love, with the greatest of these being love. Walk with Him! Be blessed!

And there were shepherds living out in the fields nearby, keeping watch over their flocks at night. An angel of the Lord appeared to them, and the glory of the Lord shone around them, and they were terrified. But the angel said to them, "Do not be afraid. I bring you good news that will cause great joy for all the people. Today in the town of David a Savior has been born to you; he is the Messiah, the Lord. This will be a sign to you: You will find a baby wrapped in cloths and lying in a manger." Suddenly a great company of the heavenly host appeared with the angel, praising God and saying, "Glory to God in the highest heaven, and on earth peace to those on whom his favor rests." When the angels had left them and gone into heaven, the shepherds said to one another, "Let's go to Bethlehem and see this thing that has happened, which the Lord has told us about." So they hurried off and found Mary and Joseph, and the baby, who was lying in the manger. When they had seen him, they spread the word concerning what had been told them about this child, and all who heard it were amazed at what the shepherds said to them. But Mary treasured up all these things and pondered them in her heart. The shepherds returned, glorifying and praising God for all the things they had heard and seen, which were just as they had been told.

—Luke 2:8–20 (NIV)

These verses are read more during the Christmas season, but I think reading them anytime of the year is an amazing reminder of the perfect plan God has for humankind, a plan to save us from our sinful nature and bring us into a perfect relationship with Him. So whatever month it may be, merry Christmas!

Walk with Him! Be blessed!

Do not withhold your mercy from me, Lord; may your love and faithfulness always protect me.

—Psalms 40:11 (NIV)

The ending of one year and the beginning of another always has us looking forward to a new beginning, a fresh beginning, or even the start of a lot of unknowns. At the same time, we look back at the missed opportunities, the unfinished stuff that now must be left unfinished because it is time to move on to new stuff. The one sure promise we have is that no matter if we are looking forward or backward, God's mercy, love, and faithfulness always surround and protect us.

Walk with Him! Be blessed!

This is how the birth of Jesus the Messiah came about: His mother Mary was pledged to be married to Joseph, but before they came together, she was found to be pregnant through the Holy Spirit. Because Joseph her husband was faithful to the law, and yet did not want to expose her to public disgrace, he had in mind to divorce her quietly. But after he had considered this, an angel of the Lord appeared to him in a dream and said, "Joseph son of David, do not be afraid to take Mary home as your wife, because what is conceived in her is from the Holy Spirit. She will give birth to a son, and you are to give him the name Jesus, because he will save his people from their sins." All this took place to fulfill what the Lord had said through the prophet: "The virgin will conceive and give birth to a son, and they will call him Immanuel" (which means "God with us"). When Joseph woke up, he did what the angel of the Lord had commanded him and took Mary home as his wife. But he did not consummate their marriage until she gave birth to a son. And he gave him the name Jesus.

—Matthew 1:18–25 (NIV)

Joseph's faith, trust, and character are amazing. Apart from these verses, there is very little mentioned about Joseph, except for when Christ was twelve and stayed back at the temple, leading Mary and Joseph to go back and get Him. After that, there is not much mention of Joseph, yet he shows us what it means to truly have faith in God and to trust in His promises and character. I mean, Joseph took in the pregnant woman he was pledged to be married to. Can you imagine what the talk was like? "Right. The child is not yours? Why have you taken her in then? You are still marrying her? If the child is not yours, you should publicly disgrace her like she did you!" (This is not from the Bible; it is just a product of my imagination.) Instead of listening to people with his ears, Joseph heard God with his heart. He believed God more than he believed people. He took God at His Word. If we were more like Joseph, we would walk with Christ more closely. Walk with Him! Be blessed!

Let us not become weary in doing good, for at the proper time we will reap a harvest if we do not give up.

—Galatians 6:9 (NIV)

Why do we do what we do? Is it because if we don't give up, eventually we will get what we want? Isn't that what this verse seems to say? From the world's perspective, that is probably true, but it isn't true from God's perspective. He provides the seeds (the gospel of Jesus Christ) we are planting. We continue planting those seeds by loving people like Christ has loved us. Eventually we will get to see the difference that the planted seeds make on those lives wherein we sowed them. That is one of the greatest harvests there could ever be, to see lives changed because of Jesus.

Walk with Him! Be blessed!

So when Martha heard that Jesus was coming, she went and met him, but Mary remained seated in the house. Martha said to Jesus, "Lord, if you had been here, my brother would not have died. But even now I know that whatever you ask from God, God will give you." Jesus said to her, "Your brother will rise again." Martha said to him, "I know that he will rise again in the resurrection on the last day."

—John 11:20–24 (ESV)

Martha said, "Jesus, if You had been here, my brother Lazarus would not have died!" In other words, she was saying, "Why weren't You here? You could have prevented this pain and hurt we are going through! You weren't here! Where were You? But You know what, Jesus? You can still fix this, right?"

Jesus says, "Lazarus will rise. Trust Me!"

Martha: "Oh, I know that he will be resurrected, Jesus. You don't have to tell me that! I am one who believes in the resurrection, remember? You are talking to Martha, the one who cooked the meal while my sister sat at Your feet. We all will rise again! But what about now? I am hurting because my brother is dead. If You had been here, we wouldn't be going through this!"

Jesus: "Where is Lazarus?"

Goodness, too often I sound much like I imagine Martha sounded. I must remember that God's ways are not my ways and how patient He is with me, because I tend to think I know how He is working when really I have such a small part to play. There is no way my thoughts and understanding can get close to Christ's understanding of what is going on around me. When I come to be okay with knowing that I know just enough to keep me seeking Him, my faith begins to grow. I can begin to rest in what I know, and I am edified in knowing that Christ has the rest of it.

Walk with Him! Be blessed!

Consider it pure joy, my brothers and sisters, whenever you face trials of many kinds, because you know that the testing of your faith produces perseverance. Let perseverance finish its work so that you may be mature and complete, not lacking anything.

—James 1:2–4 (NIV)

Whoa, hold on! We are to consider trials pure joy? But isn't that an oxymoron of sorts, mentioning trials and joy in the same breath? When we read on, this chapter of the book of James tells us why we should consider trials pure joy. Through trials we learn perseverance (steadfastness), which strengthens faith, which helps us become more mature in Christ—and through that maturity in Christ we become complete. God designed us to be lacking in nothing through His Son. We have Christ, who is the completion of God's perfect plan for us. He is the perfect example of how the end justifies the means. Walk with Him! Be blessed!

Then James and John, the sons of Zebedee, came to him. "Teacher," they said, "we want you to do for us whatever we ask." "What do you want me to do for you?" he asked. They replied, "Let one of us sit at your right and the other at your left in your glory." "You don't know what you are asking," Jesus said. "Can you drink the cup I drink or be baptized with the baptism I am baptized with?" "We can," they answered. Jesus said to them, "You will drink the cup I drink and be baptized with the baptism I am baptized with, but to sit at my right or left is not for me to grants. These places belong to those for whom they have been prepared." When the ten heard about this, they became indignant with James and John. Jesus called them together and said, "You know that those who are regarded as rulers of the Gentiles lord it over them, and their high officials exercise authority over them. Not so with you. Instead, whoever wants to become great among you must be your servant, and whoever wants to be first must be slave of all. For even the Son of Man did not come to be served, but to serve, and to give his life as a ransom for many."

—Mark 10:35–45 (NIV)

One day someone asked me, "Because I am your favorite, will you let me…?" After that, the above verse came to mind. Now, I don't have a clue what James's and John's motives were in asking Jesus about sitting next to Him in heaven, but I do know the motive of the person who asked me that question. The individual wanted special privileges because I liked him, which made me think how many times I go to Jesus with the same attitude. "Hey, Jesus, since I am one of Your 'favorites,' could You…?"

Look how unbeneficial that attitude is. When the other disciples heard of what James and John had asked, they got upset and started talking. I don't know their hearts, but what does seem apparent is that they didn't understand relationships, especially close ones. Jesus explained to them, "If you desire to be first, you must be willing to be last [the low man on the totem pole]." He reminded them, "I came to serve, not to be served." Being someone's favorite (it is a good thing we are all Jesus's favorites!) doesn't mean we get to slack or are given special privileges. It means we give of ourselves more for the One of whom we are the "favorite."

Walk with Him! Be blessed!

No power in the sky above or in the earth below—indeed, nothing in all creation will ever be able to separate us from the love of God that is revealed in Christ Jesus our Lord.

—Romans 8:39 (NLT)

No matter how alone you may feel, you are never separated from God's love. Wherever you go, Christ's love surrounds you. Take some time today to hear His footsteps that are going before you, beside you, and behind you. He is there! You just need to remember that we walk with Him. Be blessed!

May the God who gives endurance and encouragement give you the same attitude of mind toward each other that Christ Jesus had, so that with one mind and one voice you may glorify the God and Father of our Lord Jesus Christ.

—Romans 15:5–6 (NIV)

Life would be so grand if we could truly live with the attitude that our minds are like Christ's. Jesus lived to serve others, to the point of dying on the cross. Unfortunately, in the world serving others isn't seen as very beneficial. I mean, if we put others' needs and wants before our own, then that must mean we will have to do with less, right? Doesn't sacrificing mean going without what we want, and not having our way so someone else can? The verse above points us to the Source of our endurance and encouragement, which is God the Father. Only by going to the Father and letting Him change us can we even begin to have the heart of Christ, a heart that serves without wondering what it is going to cost or, better yet, that lets God bring us to the place of knowing exactly what it will cost us and we are still willing to do it. If we have this attitude, then, with one mind and one voice (like Christ), we will glorify God, the Father of our Lord and Savior, Jesus Christ, who is the very reason we were created. Walk with Him! Be blessed!

Not that I have already obtained this or am already perfect, but I press on to make it my own, because Christ Jesus has made me his own. Brothers, I do not consider that I have made it my own. But one thing I do: forgetting what lies behind and straining forward to what lies ahead, I press on toward the goal for the prize of the upward call of God in Christ Jesus.

—Philippians 3:12–14 (ESV)

Wow, a lot is packed into these verses. Paul is saying many things. First: I have accepted Christ as my Lord and Savior, but I am not perfect. I am not there yet, but I am headed in a new direction with Christ. Second: I am on my own path. My life with Christ is not going to look like anyone else's. It is my own, the one for which He died so I could live it out for Him, because I am His. All along the way, I remember that I have not arrived yet, so I must remain in the shadow of Christ, who goes before me in all I do. Third: the past is just that—the past. It is no longer *my* past, because Christ made me a new creation when He became Lord and Savior of my life. So I no longer have a past to hold onto, to get over, or to undo or fix before moving on. It is time to get up, let go, look forward, and let God have my fully surrendered heart so I can press on toward the goal of living the life that Christ died for.

How about you? Are you ready to let go of something that is no longer there, namely, your past, and press on toward the new life Christ died for so that you could have it?

Walk with Him! Be blessed!

Jesus sat down opposite the place where the offerings were put and watched the crowd putting their money into the temple treasury. Many rich people threw in large amounts. But a poor widow came and put in two very small copper coins, worth only a few cents. Calling his disciples to him, Jesus said, "Truly I tell you, this poor widow has put more into the treasury than all the others. They all gave out of their wealth; but she, out of her poverty, put in everything—all she had to live on."

—Mark 12:41–44 (NIV)

Does it ever seem as if you have nothing else to give to God or others? Do you seem to have so little left (money, time, or energy) that you are afraid to give it up? You wonder if you do give it, then what will be left for you? How can you help others if you yourself are totally bankrupt in many areas of your life? Maybe what this verse is saying is that Jesus will take the gift of two small coins and multiply them out of His overflow because He more than anyone else and He understands giving everything you have to God so that the Father can do only what He can do! Whatever you have left, give it to Him who manages all things well. Walk with Him! Be blessed!

Act wisely toward outsiders, making the most of the opportunity. Your speech should always be gracious and sprinkled with insight so that you may know how to respond to every person.

—Colossians 4:5–6 (CEB)

I don't have anything to add to something so plainly said. Act wisely, and don't miss an opportunity to share Jesus with a hurting world. Speak graciously, and stay covered with prayer so what you say to the person you are speaking to will be blessed.

Walk with Him! Be blessed yourself!

> But blessed is the one who trusts in the Lord, whose confidence is in him. They will be like a tree planted by the water that sends out its roots by the stream. It does not fear when heat comes; its leaves are always green. It has no worries in a year of drought and never fails to bear fruit.
>
> —Jeremiah 17:7–8 (NIV)

Even when life is dry and we are overwhelmed by the heat of our circumstances, when everything is parched from the absence of fresh drink, and when life isn't going smoothly for us, if we are rooted in Christ we will not only be sustained but also we will be different from our surroundings! We will be able to bless others and show them that it is not where one's trunk is visible that matters. It is where one's roots are planted that makes a difference in life.

Walk with Him! Be blessed!

When I was a child, I talked like a child, I thought like a child, I reasoned like a child. When I became a man, I put the ways of childhood behind me. For now we see only a reflection as in a mirror; then we shall see face to face. Now I know in part; then I shall know fully, even as I am fully known. And now these three remain: faith, hope and love. But the greatest of these is love.

—1 Corinthians 13:11–13 (NIV)

One time when I came out of the gym after working out, I saw that a fog had rolled in. As I drove closer to my house, the fog got thicker and more dense, which brought the above verse to my mind. Sometimes, even on the most familiar road, things get unclear and foggy, but we are encouraged to continue growing and maturing in Christ. We may never fully understand everything in life, but faith, hope, and love give us a better understanding of what life in Christ may be. The greatest thing we can do is to love like we are loved by Christ. Walk with Him! Be blessed!

For God is not a God of confusion, but of peace. As in all the churches of the saints.

—1 Corinthians 14:33 (ASV)

We live in a world of so many mixed messages that confusion has become a very normal part of life. This is not how God intended us to live. He designed the world with much structure and order, separating day from night and season from season. In Ecclesiastes, Solomon speaks about everything's having its season, a beginning and an end, and structure and order. The world's message says, "Live by the seat of your pants. And by the way, parents, don't stymie the creativity in your children by preventing them from running as they wish with no boundaries." This is in stark contrast to God's design, which offers peace if we stay away from confusion and disorder. How do we change? Little by little, start by introducing some type of small structure into your day, whether it be reading the Word or going to the gym. Yes, you may have to get up fifteen to twenty minutes earlier, but if it will get you on the path toward a more peaceful life, then it will be well worth it. If I can minimize confusion and have peace, I am willing to do what it takes to achieve this. My hope is to become more aware of the presence of God in my life by receiving the peace that surpasses all understanding. How about you?

Walk with Him! Be blessed!

This is my command—be strong and courageous! Do not be afraid or discouraged. For the Lord your God is with you wherever you go.

—Joshua 1:9 (NLT)

We know God is always with us. He promises never to leave or forsake us. So why do we feel abandoned so often? Maybe it is because while God is ever present in our lives, it is we who aren't the present ones. We get so caught up in where we are going and in looking back at where we have been that we miss right where we are, which is exactly where we are called to be strong and courageous. Maybe when we start being present, strong, and courageous right where we are, we will realize that the Lord our God is with us right where we are.

Walk with Him! Be blessed!

The Lord is close to the brokenhearted; he saves those whose spirits are crushed. The righteous have many problems, but the Lord delivers them from every one.

—Psalms 34:18–19 (CEB)

Wow! It appears that even in Old Testament days, people were desiring a life without problems. Why else would the Lord tell them that the righteous would have problems but that He would be with them through those times, acting as their deliver? Jesus came, as described in the New Testament, to be the righteousness we all need so we can stand in the presence of the holy God Almighty. Giving our life to Christ does not a "fix" this life's problems, as many people are hoping. He is so much more than a fixer. He is the peace that surpasses all understanding. When we feel alone, He promises never to leave or forsake us. Yes, He came to give us life and life more abundantly, but we must remember that God's ways are not our ways. God is not confined to our way of thinking. He is God. What is it we know? We know His promise that whatever our life hands out to us, He will be there. He goes all the way with us, protecting us, guiding us, and whispering in our ear, telling us, "I am here! My love for you is bigger than anything that is happening. I died on the cross for you. I won't leave you during this trial." Know that the Lord your God is in your midst. The mighty One will save you. Walk with Him! Be blessed!

May these words of my mouth and this meditation of my heart
be pleasing in your sight, Lord, my Rock and my Redeemer.

—Psalms 19:14 (NIV)

In this day of saying anything on our mind, posting a response to what has
been posted online or tweeting something in order to get a response, we
tend to forget the One we are living to please. Before our next response, or
even before the beginning of responses to come, may we stop and think,
*Is this pleasing to You, Lord? Will these words or this post or tweet be pleasing
in your sight, O Lord?* Do what you do for an audience of one. Walk with
Him! Be blessed!

> Don't be conformed to the patterns of this world, but be transformed by the renewing of your minds so that you can figure out what God's will is—what is good and pleasing and mature. ... Don't hesitate to be enthusiastic—be on fire in the Spirit as you serve the Lord! Be happy in your hope, stand your ground when you're in trouble, and devote yourselves to prayer.
>
> —Romans 12:2, 11–12 (CEB)

Don't be comfortable with the things of this world? Ouch! But I like some things of this world. Exactly, but is it worth it if things of this world stand between me and my relationship with Christ? We must renew our mind in the things of Christ so that we will know the difference between what we should be okay with in our lives and what we should not be okay with.

Love the Lord your God with all your heart, and speak of Him to others.

When things go awry in your life, don't move and don't run. Instead, go to the Word—and pray without ceasing.

Walk with Him! Be blessed!

Have you not known? Have you not heard? The Lord is the everlasting God, the Creator of the ends of the earth. He does not faint or grow weary; his understanding is unsearchable. He gives power to the faint, and to him who has no might he increases strength. Even youths shall faint and be weary, and young men shall fall exhausted; but they who wait for the Lord shall renew their strength; they shall mount up with wings like eagles; they shall run and not be weary; they shall walk and not faint.

—Isaiah 40:28–31 (ESV)

I read Bible verses while working out, and I love it when this verse rolls around. Each time it appears, it gives me renewed strength to finish and not quit, especially on those days when it is simply not easy to continue. Some days are just hard. The easy thing to do is to just quit, stay in bed, get angry, and make other people's lives miserable so I won't be alone in my misery. But God's Word tells me (as I paraphrase it), "Yes, you will get tired. No, it won't always be easy. But if you will wait on Me, I will be your Source of renewal. And just as if you were mounted on the wings of an eagle, you will see things from a higher-up perspective." With these words, the verse isn't just saying, "Hold on. Life will get better"; I believe it is promising us an understanding of our life from God's perspective, where He is above all.

Walk with Him! Be blessed!

For the word of God is living and active, sharper than any two-edged sword, piercing to the division of soul and of spirit, of joints and of marrow, and discerning the thoughts and intentions of the heart.

—Hebrews 4:12 (ESV)

Man, the Word doesn't mess around, does it? Forget how we try to dress up our lives to make them look good. The Word goes straight to where it all begins: the heart. I'm not talking about the muscle that beats inside the human chest but about the soul, the spirit. We might be able to hide what is going on inside of us from people, but we can't hide it from God. And really, why would we not want to have the comfort of being completely honest with God, who is the Creator and Sustainer of life? What a wonderful thing to know we can be completely honest with Him who already knows. We don't have to hide behind smiles, hold back tears, or control our anger when we take it to the One who already knows. The interesting thing is that when I do get honest with Christ, what I say to Him always comes back to me as not quite as bad as I had thought it would be (which makes me think of the peace that surpasses all understanding). My mess isn't as messy as I thought it was. My hurt and anger are easier to deal with as well. Wow, honesty really is the best policy. Be honest with Him who already knows. Walk with Him! Be blessed!

Every scripture is inspired by God and is useful for teaching, for showing mistakes, for correcting, and for training character, so that the person who belongs to God can be equipped to do everything that is good.

—2 Timothy 3:16–17 (CEB)

People at one learned to read using the Bible, God's Word. Whether they wanted it to be or not, the Bible was a part of their life. Maybe that is why C. S. Lewis in his book *Mere Christianity* asked the question, "How does man seem to be born with a sense of just and unjust?" I believe it is because the Word of God was once present in people's everyday life. Whether people realized it or not, it was also present in their being. Over the course of time, the Word has been pushed and shoved into smaller parts of people's lives. To have it in one's life today, it has to be presented, which is a wonderful opportunity for us Christians. What a blessing to get to share Christ with a hurting world. The problem is that many of us are reminded daily how inadequate our knowledge of the Word is, so we tend to back off from sharing it, feeling as if we don't have all the answers. Don't let that stop you from sharing the Word. Share the fact that there is only one answer to life—Jesus—and just encourage people to start reading the Word. It is a double-edged sword and cuts through anything we don't understand. In time the Word becomes a part of who we are, and through living it out we will begin to understand it.

Walk with Him! Be blessed!

I have stored up your word in my heart that I might not sin against you. Blessed are you, O Lord; teach me your statutes!

—Psalms 119:11–12 (ESV)

Some mornings I awake and have such a desire to follow God's Word that I am almost paralyzed with fear of sinning against God. I mean, doing nothing would be better than doing something wrong, right? (Stick with me.) Other mornings when I awake, my heart doesn't think about anything but what it wants to do, so I start running amok after putting my feet on the floor. Hey, doing something wrong is better than doing nothing, right? Well, actually, neither is the way God desires us to live. He doesn't want us to live in fear of messing up. Guilt and condemnation are not from Him. At the same time, He doesn't want us to follow every fleshly desire, because He already knows the consequences of living that way, which are guilt and condemnation. So either way we end up at the same place if we choose to live in fear of disappointment or in selfishness, seeking after our own desires. What, then, do we do? Just like it says, "Store the Word in your heart so you will know what is pleasing to the Lord." Let God teach you daily. Walk with Him! Be blessed!

But to you who are listening I say: Love your enemies, do good to those who hate you, bless those who curse you, pray for those who mistreat you. If someone slaps you on one cheek, turn to them the other also. If someone takes your coat, do not withhold your shirt from them. Give to everyone who asks you, and if anyone takes what belongs to you, do not demand it back. Do to others as you would have them do to you. If you love those who love you, what credit is that to you? Even sinners love those who love them. And if you do good to those who are good to you, what credit is that to you? Even sinners do that. And if you lend to those from whom you expect repayment, what credit is that to you? Even sinners lend to sinners, expecting to be repaid in full. But love your enemies, do good to them, and lend to them without expecting to get anything back. Then your reward will be great, and you will be children of the Most High, because he is kind to the ungrateful and wicked. Be merciful, just as your Father is merciful.

—Luke 6:27–36 (NIV)

The above verses quote Jesus speaking to a crowd of people, which I bet (I am not a gambling person; I'm just using the phrase) was a lot like a crowd that would be gathered today—people desiring and looking for something better than what the world has to offer. Yet what Jesus said was probably much different from what the crowd had been expecting to hear.

How many of us know there is something better out there yet aren't able to look past what we know? Jesus offers us something different from what the world offers. The question is, are we willing to be different from what we know?

Walk with Him! Be blessed!

But the one who did not know, and did what deserved a beating, will receive a light beating. Everyone to whom much was given, of him much will be required, and from him to whom they entrusted much, they will demand the more.

—Luke 12:48 (ESV)

I keep thinking of the Israelites when I read this verse. What comes to mind is, I bet they were totally confused and shocked when, after all the years they had spent in the wilderness and once it came time to enter the Promised Land, there was still fighting to be done. If I were in their place, I would have been shocked and confused. I probably would have even argued the point: "Hey, God, we just wandered out here for forty years. Haven't we earned the right to just walk in and have the Promised Land? You mean You expect more from us?" And God probably would have responded with, "Hey, you of little understanding, I said 'Promised Land,' not 'the garden of Eden.' Ask a farmer: land requires work and upkeep. Yes, I want you to be a part of the process of taking the Promised Land as yours. And through that, I will continue to show you that you are Mine."

How many times do we just want the blessings of God and not the responsibility of those blessings? The bigger the responsibility, the more opportunity we have to continue to see God work. That is why "to those who have been given much, much will be required" is a good thing. The more God can trust you with, the more you can trust Him. Wow, I love how God works!

Walk with Him! Be blessed!

In the beginning, God created the heavens and the earth. The earth was without form and void, and darkness was over the face of the deep. And the Spirit of God was hovering over the face of the waters. And God said, "Let there be light," and there was light. And God saw that the light was good. And God separated the light from the darkness. God called the light Day, and the darkness he called Night. And there was evening and there was morning, the first day.

—Genesis 1:1–5 (ESV)

At one time, what is described above was the accepted theory of the origin of the earth. The idea of life as a divine creation was not widely questioned. It was what made sense (not the best word to use, but it is the only one I have) when considering life as it was in the fifteenth century BC, with so much information yet to be learned. To believe in divine creation was much easier some time ago than it might be now, as now there are many thoughts about and explanations of how life came into being.

A belief in divine creation is the basis of a belief in the *real* foundation of the gospel of Jesus Christ, because God's perfect plan of salvation through Christ began with His creation of life and of time. He began life with Christ's life in mind, knowing that all things before Christ would lead to Him and that all things after Christ would come from Him who gave His life. To believe in divine creation from the start to His finish (the second coming of Christ) is easy, even with other ideas out there. For me it is the only thing that makes sense. (Hmm, I guess that wasn't such a bad use of that word after all.)

Walk with Him! Be blessed!

Then Jesus said to them, "Give back to Caesar what is Caesar's and to God what is God's." And they were amazed at him.

—Mark 12:17 (NIV)

Every year, tax season rolls around. Most years I put off paying my taxes until April 15. I don't even get the required documents to my accountant until the middle or end of March. And even though I try not to think about taxes, the fact that it is tax time is often on my mind (which I consider to be a burden). This year, bam! I got my taxes done and over with as early as I could. Once I had finished, I thought, *Ha-ha! Give unto Caesar what is Caesar's. Well, there you go, Caesar. I don't have to mess with you for another year.* Then I remembered the rest of the verse quoted above: "Give unto God what is God's." It hit me in a lot of ways. For example, I treat God like I treat taxes: "Okay, there, I paid You. I gave You what is Yours. Now am I done until next year."

Oh, Lord, forgive me. You are so much more than a tax collector. Forgive me when my heart has regarded you as less than You are. Thank You, Lord, for forgiving me when I am wrong.

I love it when the Lord gives me one of these heart-check moments.

Walk with Him! Be blessed!

For because he himself has suffered when tempted, he is able to help those who are being tempted.

—Hebrews 2:18 (ESV)

Jesus gets it. He really does! While on earth, He faced every temptation there was to face. So when you feel like no one understands what you are going through, read the Word and you will see that Jesus does understand. He walked a very similar path you are walking right now—and then some. He put on the shoes of total life, giving His life as a sacrifice on the cross to defeat death so you could live forever with Him and God the Father. He was so burdened with His life's calling that He sweated blood from His brow before going to the cross. He asked, "Are you sure, Father, that this is the only way Your will can be done?" And then He said, "Okay. Let's do this Your way, not Mine. You are Father God." If only we could willingly get on the cross daily and say, "Your will, Father." That would be a way to truly walk with Him.

Be blessed!

Cast your cares on the Lord and he will sustain you; he will never let the righteous be shaken.

—Psalms 55:22 (NIV)

When trouble comes and we get to the point of saying, "I guess all we can do is trust God," and we start quoting all the Scriptures we can find on trusting Him who will get us through, we feel pretty good about ourselves because we are trusting God, right? Really, what we have done is to have tried everything else we knew to do and then, when that didn't work, gone to God to fix our problem, like He is our last line of defense, our last resort. It is as if we don't know what else to do but to say, "Okay, I will trust You, God. Nothing else works, so I guess I will give You a try."

Trusting God is not something we should do as a last resort. It is something we should do as a first resort. It is a *privilege* to know that He is faithful to the point of dying for us. So, in all things, trusting God is an honor, a privilege, and not a last thing to be tried when nothing else has worked. Trusting God should be the first thing we do in the morning, and then we should continue doing it all throughout the day and even during the night while we sleep. We can trust Christ with every aspect of our life. He will sustain us. The righteous (His children) will never be shaken.

Walk with Him! Be blessed!

But Peter and the apostles answered, "We must obey God rather than men."

—Acts 5:29 (ESV)

Have you ever stood at a crossroads in life and heard the world saying, "Go to the left. It makes the most sense. See, this is how it can all work out. Notice that the other path is much more bumpy and rocky—and look at all the trees and bushes you will have to deal with if you go down that path. Oh, man, do you see that hill up ahead? Pretty steep! Look at the path to the left. It is nice and flat, with not many trees, so you can see much farther down the road. It provides a much better line of sight," when you know in your heart that the path to the right is the one you are called to walk? The extra foliage will provide protection from the elements and shade from the hot sun. Those bushes might provide fruit for your meals. Who knows what you will find under the rocks you have to move. And that steep hill? Can you say, "Good cardio workout"? Faith comes from hearing the Word of God. "Thanks for your input, world, but I will go to the right."

Walk with Him! Be blessed!

Glory in his holy name; let the hearts of those who seek the Lord rejoice. Look to the Lord and his strength; seek his face always.

—1 Chronicles 16:10–11 (NIV)

The world says that strong people do not need anyone or anything. But God designed us for dependence on Him. A true sign of strength is admitting we need more than ourselves. We need a Savior whose name is Jesus. Dependence on Christ is God's perfect plan for us. We are to be completely dependent on the One who gave His life for us. God's desire is that we depend on Him for His strength.

Walk with Him! Be blessed!

Thy word is a lamp unto my feet, And light unto my path.

—Psalms 119:105 (ASV)

When I was a kid, on a fifth grade field trip, we went to the alabaster caverns in northwest Oklahoma. During the tour of the cave, the tour guide would turn off the lights to show us what total darkness was. I mean, it was totally dark. While the lights were off, the guides told us that if a person stayed in total darkness long enough, then he or she would go blind.

Coming out of the cave, my eyes took time to adjust to the sunlight, something I was used to being in. Yet the short time I had spent without the sunlight made the light feel uncomfortable for a while. So it is no wonder that when we as sinners are coming out of the darkness of sin into the Light of Christ our hearts have a hard time adjusting to the *Son*shine, especially those who have been in darkness for so long that they are almost blind. It is an interesting thing to be blinded by darkness, not by light. We must stay in the Word of God so that we are constantly in the light that the Word provides. Soon we will stop having to adjust to the Light (Christ), because we will be able to live in the Light.

Walk with Him! Be blessed!

You know that in a race all the runners run but only one wins the prize, don't you? You must run in such a way that you may be victorious.

—1 Corinthians 9:24 (ESV)

As a runner, I run on a treadmill because I like to exercise in a controlled environment. No wind or cold for me. Okay, so some may consider me a wimpy runner. Nonetheless, I run. And I have gotten really good at it. I mean, I even run with my eyes closed some (sounds crazy, I know, but try doing that outside). One day I was running with my eyes closed and I would periodically open them. When I was doing that, the following thought came to me. In life, the "race" we are running can seem like running on a treadmill. The scenery may not change much. We go to the same place to work, see the same people, attend events with the same people, and attend church and see the same people. If we aren't careful, we will get so used to running through our days, doing what we do, that we will miss meeting other people and encountering opportunities to be used by God. We can't change our route in life all the time, but we can ask God to change our heart and eyes so we can see the path on which we are running in a different way. And with our eyes and heart being able to see differently, the same path will look different and the treadmill of life can be run in victory.

Walk with Him! Be blessed!

After the Sabbath, at dawn on the first day of the week, Mary Magdalene and the other Mary went to look at the tomb. There was a violent earthquake, for an angel of the Lord came down from heaven and, going to the tomb, rolled back the stone and sat on it. His appearance was like lightning, and his clothes were white as snow. The guards were so afraid of him that they shook and became like dead men. The angel said to the women, "Do not be afraid, for I know that you are looking for Jesus, who was crucified. He is not here; he has risen, just as he said. Come and see the place where he lay. Then go quickly and tell his disciples: 'He has risen from the dead and is going ahead of you into Galilee. There you will see him.' Now I have told you." So the women hurried away from the tomb, afraid yet filled with joy, and ran to tell his disciples. Suddenly Jesus met them. "Greetings," he said. They came to him, clasped his feet and worshiped him. Then Jesus said to them, "Do not be afraid. Go and tell my brothers to go to Galilee; there they will see me."

—Matthew 23:1–10 (NIV)

All hope had been ripped away when people witnessed Christ's death on the cross. Then in a matter of a few just-as-confusing moments, hope was restored. I love how Christ's instructions were very plain and simple: "Go and tell, and you will see. And by the way, there is no need to fear." I love how He still, more than two thousand years later, is instructing us to "go and tell" so we will see and not fear. Christ is alive and with us. When we go, He is with us. When we speak, He sometimes speaks through us. When we see, He allows us to see through His eyes. When we are fearful, He gives us His boldness and courage. We just need to follow His simple instructions to "go, tell, and see." Oh, and don't take fear with you.

Walk with Him! Be blessed!

> For the grace of God has appeared that offers salvation to all people. It teaches us to say "No" to ungodliness and worldly passions, and to live self-controlled, upright and godly lives in this present age, while we wait for the blessed hope—the appearing of the glory of our great God and Savior, Jesus Christ.

—Titus 2:11–13 (NIV)

Instruction on how to live is found throughout the Word. Unfortunately, people today question if we can actually live out these instructions. The world and the things of this world make it seem almost impossible to live a godly life. I mean, really, can one remain a virgin until marriage? Can one really be honest in work, with friends, and on tax forms? Can we really put God first, others second, and ourselves third? The answer to all of these questions is yes. And God's Word tells us that it is so, as follows:

- "I can do all things through Christ who strengthens me" (Philippians 4:13)!
- "Jesus looked at them and said, 'With man this is impossible, but with God all things are possible'" (Mathew 19:26).
- "No temptation has overtaken you except what is common to mankind. And God is faithful; he will not let you be tempted beyond what you can bear. But when you are tempted, he will also provide a way out so that you can endure it" (1 Corinthians 10:13).

You see, not only does God give us instructions on how to live life in a way that honors Christ, but also we are given the promise that "the Lord himself goes before you and will be with you; he will never leave you nor forsake you. Do not be afraid; do not be discouraged" (Deuteronomy 31:8). Not only does God's Word provide instruction, but also it gives us promises that we will be able to carry out those instructions because God is with us every step of the way. We just need to walk with Him.

Be blessed!

Where your treasure is, there your heart will be too.

—Luke 12:34 (CEB)

When our daughter was in sixth grade, she did gymnastics, which required getting up on Saturdays very early to compete at gymnastics meets. One Sunday morning after her Saturday of competition, I went in to wake her for Sunday school and church. For one moment my thought was, *Oh, she is tired from yesterday, Just let her sleep.* In the next moment, my thought was, *You woke her for gymnastics, but you won't wake her for Jesus? What does that tell her about what you value?!* Wow, it wasn't about going to Sunday school and church anymore; it was about what my choices were telling my children I treasured: things of this world or things of Christ? By my choices, they were able to see my heart. What you value tells everyone where your heart is. Let's just say that this verse took on a whole new meaning for me that day.

Walk with Him! Be blessed!

I am going to try to share something that, besides the Word of God, has had the most impact on my relationship with Christ. I will share it in the way I heard it so that nothing will be lost in the translation. This is what I heard from brother Johnny Tims (a big bear of a man of God):

Jesus: Johnny, do you love Me?

Johnny: Of course, Lord, I love You!

Jesus: Johnny, are you sure? I know you preach My Word and share My gospel. You take care of the sick, needy, and poor. But do you love Me?

Johnny: Of course, Lord, I love You!

Jesus: Thank you, Johnny, for your assurance of your love for Me, but, Johnny, heaven is full. When you die you won't be going there! [Now this will never happen, but stay with me.] Does your love for Me go beyond the promise of heaven? Has experiencing My love, which I died to show you, go beyond the promise of heaven?

Wow, what a question! I had to ask myself what my answer would be or, better yet, what my life would look like if heaven wasn't promised to me. Have I allowed Christ's love to make such a difference in my life that it was enough? Christ's love is available and present in the lives of all, even those who choose not to receive His free gift of grace. This moment of my life made me realize, "Better is one day in your courts than a thousand elsewhere; I would rather be a doorkeeper in the house of my God than dwell in the tents of the wicked" (Psalms 84:10)!

Walk with Him! Be blessed!

When he had received the drink, Jesus said, "It is finished."
With that, he bowed his head and gave up his spirit.

—John 19:30 (NIV)

Wait. Hold on. "It is finished"? Then what have I been doing these last three years? I gave up a job; my family thinks I am crazy; and the important people of this country want to hurt me, and You just said, "It is finished"? I can only imagine what Christ's followers were thinking when they thought He had just "given up" on the cross. Yes, Jesus "gave up" (His Spirit), but not in the way His followers probably thought. Unfortunately they, just like us, weren't good listeners. Jesus said "It is finished," not "It has ended."

Before going to the cross, Jesus told His disciples what was coming, but they didn't want to hear it. Then Jesus said, "After three days I will return from the dead" (cf. "I will rebuild the temple in three days"). But they didn't hear that either.

Jesus said "It is finished" so the life He came to give us could begin. Walk with Him! Be blessed!

> Now I am happy, not because you were made sad, but because your sorrow made you decide to change. That is what God wanted, so you were not hurt by us in any way. The kind of sorrow God wants makes people decide to change their lives. This leads them to salvation, and we cannot be sorry for that. But the kind of sorrow the world has will bring death.

—2 Corinthians 7:9–10 (ERV)

The above is from a letter Paul wrote to the people of the church at Corinth. Evidently what had previously been said wasn't all lovey-dovey, because in this part of the letter he is saying that it (whatever it was) had made them sad and that he was glad about it. Whoa, that doesn't sound nice! But what he was saying is that their sorrow made them want to change, and for that he was happy. Too many times we feel bad for what we have done, but not bad enough to change. My mom (who is a wise woman; if she had written the letter to the church, it probably would have been even more harsh), when correcting me after I was called out and felt sorry about what I had done, would ask, "Are you really sorry, or are you just sorry that you got caught? If you are really sorry, then you won't do it again [i.e., you'll be moved to change], but if you're just sorry you got caught, then we will be having this conversation again." When you have been corrected by the Holy Spirit, are you moved to change or will you be having that conversation again?

Walk with Him! Be blessed!

And He said to them, Go into all the world and preach and publish openly the good news [the Gospel] to every creature [of the whole human race].

—Mark 16:15 (AB)

One day I was walking down a hill and saw a big turtle. Someone who had stopped, had gotten out of his car, and was picking up the turtle. When I passed, the person said, "I am going to move him so he doesn't get run over!"

Instantly the thought came to me: *There are a lot of people who are in the middle of a very busy highway called life. And if someone doesn't help them, they are going to get "run over."*

People need Jesus. We who know Him must share His love with others so they can be moved to a much safer place.

Walk with Him! Be blessed!

Therefore, as you received Christ Jesus the Lord, so walk in him, rooted and built up in him and established in the faith, just as you were taught, abounding in thanksgiving. See to it that no one takes you captive by philosophy and empty deceit, according to human tradition, according to the elemental spirits of the world, and not according to Christ.

—Colossians 2:6–8 (ESV)

I gave this verse to Kara (our youngest daughter) at the end of her senior year of high school. She was going off to college, where I knew she would be exposed to many ideas, thoughts, and, well, *activities* she had not been exposed to before. This verse was something I wanted her to have so as to remind her of what she had been taught. My husband, Ted, and I had been blessed to have three main places where Kara spent 90 percent of her time while growing up: Twist and Shout All-Star Cheer Gym (shout-out to Orson and all of Kara's coaches), Sooner Tumbling (shout-out to Coach Stewart and Donna), and Kanakuk Kamps (shout-out to all of Kara's counselors and the staff). (I can't thank those people enough, by the way.) These three amazing places literally helped my husband and me to raise Kara (not just her, but all three wonderful daughters we are blessed with).

You see, Ted and I knew that when Kara went to practice or spent time at camp she was being taught the same things she was being taught at home. We didn't have to undo or explain anything these other places were teaching because they and my husband and I were partners in raising her. I say this to encourage you to take an inventory of where your children are spending their time. Is what you are teaching them in the home getting reinforced in the places where they are allowed to spend their time, so that when they go off to college or into the work world they have something to pull from? I am not saying to pull them out of an activity if you realize they are being exposed to something different, but I do encourage you to have conversations about the differences and teach them to compare what the world is teaching them to what the Word of God says. Do this so that as they grow, they come to know and believe the Word so that they can remember what they have been taught when the world tries to tell them something different.

Walk with Him! Be blessed!

So, if you think you are standing firm, be careful that you don't fall!

—1 Corinthians 10:12 (NIV)

This verse jumped out at me. I am not sure why, except to say that maybe I am becoming too comfortable in some unknown area of my life that at one time was a problem that had been "fixed," so I haven't guarded my heart from it in a while and it is about to rear its ugly head again. Or maybe I just needed to be reminded that I will never become so spiritually fit that I will be strong enough to stand alone without Christ in anything or anyplace. Whatever the reason for this verse's jumping out at me, I have been reminded that I was once in need of a Savior because of my sin and that now, daily, I need a Savior so I can be saved from myself.

Walk with Him! Be blessed!

Trust in the Lord with all your heart, and do not lean on your own understanding. In all your ways acknowledge him, and he will make straight your paths.

—Proverbs 3:5–6 (ESV)

One day while driving from Billings, Montana, to Missoula, Montana, I realized how familiar the roads of Oklahoma are to me. Now, granted, I have not driven on all the roads of the great state, but the ones I have driven—from Altus to the northeast corner; from Woodward to Chickasha; and every road in between—are ones I know very well. I know almost every curve and every corner, so the drive happens almost automatically, like the car could be put on autopilot and I could just sit back and ride. Well, in Montana that day, the road I was driving was completely unfamiliar to me. I would see a curve ahead and wouldn't know if once I got there I would be turning left or right. The hills (mountains) left me wondering what the other side had to offer. It was definitely new territory.

All during the drive, the verse above kept repeating in my heart. "Trust in the Lord with all your heart. Lean not on your own I understanding." (Don't become so familiar with where you have traveled or are traveling that you are now on autopilot and your understanding of life is getting in the way of the Lord's direction for your life.) "In all your ways acknowledge Him and He will make your pathway straight." If you let others know in whom you put your trust, then every new curve or hill that lies ahead will be like a drive in west Kansas (where one can see for miles), because you know who actually has the wheel.

Walk (ride) with Him! Be blessed!

If then you have been raised with Christ, seek the things that are above, where Christ is, seated at the right hand of God. Set your minds on things that are above, not on things that are on earth.

—Colossians 3:1–2 (ESV)

Driving through Lolo, Montana, one day, I saw a sign that read, "Run the race with eternity in the view," and the verse above popped into my head, because that is what it is saying. Eternity is what is up ahead. Not the next decision I make, the next job I take, or the place where I live, but heaven is what is up ahead. Decisions and jobs are the things along the side of the road I am on. Do I need to make stops along the way? Absolutely. Do I stay in some places longer than I should? Do I dwell on things a little too much in one area? Do I sometimes think that where I am is where my race ends? Yes to all of the above. But, praise Jesus, I am wrong on all accounts, because eternity is always in my view. And that is my final destination. Woo-hoo!

Walk with Him! Be blessed!

So do not fear, for I am with you; do not be dismayed, for I am your God. I will strengthen you and help you; I will uphold you with my righteous right hand.

—Isaiah 41:10 (NIV)

The fear of the Lord is the beginning of knowledge, but fools despise wisdom and instruction.

—Proverbs 1:7 (NIV)

Wait, am I to fear or not? In the book of Isaiah, God tells us not to fear or be afraid, and then in Proverbs He tells us that in our fear is where we begin to have wisdom. I am confused, but not really. The first fear is a worldly fear, fear because we don't know what is ahead, fear because things are out of control, fear because we know we have messed up and life just seems hopeless and scary at times. The second fear is an in-awe kind of fear, a "Wow, God is our God, isn't He?" type of fear. This fear marks a beginning to our understanding that God is who He has allowed us to see. So even though these two verses, when taken collectively, may seem to be saying, "Don't fear. No, do fear," they are actually saying the same thing: don't be afraid of the things of this world or of what this world tries to do to you or around you. You should realize that your hope, security, and future are in the hands of the Almighty God who is, who was, and who is to come, and then you should put that knowledge into practice.

Walk with Him! Be blessed!

So do not fear, for I am with you; do not be dismayed, for I am your God. I will strengthen you and help you; I will uphold you with my righteous right hand.

—Isaiah 41:10 (NIV)

I wrote this on a cloudy, humid day with no sign of the sun coming out or breaking through. As a matter of fact, storms, possibly severe storms, were predicted for later in the day. It is a crazy thing that even though we don't see the sun, it is present behind the clouds. It will even be present during any storms that develop. The sun is always shining, even from the other side of the world, from where it gives light that reflects off the moon at night. This is a wonderful reminder to us that the Son is always present no matter the things that appear to be blocking Him in our life. Christ is always present, even in the storms that develop. So the next time you feel alone and think that Christ has left you, remember His promise, "I will never leave you nor forsake you." Behind the clouds, still shining is Him in His glory, preparing the beautiful rainbow that comes after some of the stormiest weather. Walk with Him! Be blessed!

If any of you lacks wisdom, you should ask God, who gives generously to all without finding fault, and it will be given to you. But when you ask, you must believe and not doubt, because the one who doubts is like a wave of the sea, blown and tossed by the wind. That person should not expect to receive anything from the Lord.

—James 1:5–7 (NIV)

I think that sometimes we confuse wisdom with wants. I know I do. I want something specific to come to pass, so I pray for it. I believe, don't doubt, and wait, and then, man, my team does not win the game. "But, Father God, you promised that if I asked and believed, I would receive." When something like this happens, is it an "unanswered" prayer or does it show my misunderstanding of the Word? The verse above makes me believe that it is my confusion about what God promises in His Word. I am not promised to get what I want, but God does promise to give me wisdom if I ask Him for it and truly believe in the Truth He reveals to me through prayer, through His Word, and through other believers speaking into my life.

God wants to give us wisdom so we won't be tossed about by the happenings of life. Now we are promised in Psalm 37:4, "Take delight in the Lord, and he will give you the desires of your heart." But that doesn't mean we get what we *want*. It does mean that our heart's desires will line up with God's will when we delight in God's ways, which comes from the wisdom God gives us generously when we ask for it. He gives us wisdom enough to understand that there are times when we won't understand.

Walk with Him! Be blessed!

That is why I am suffering as I am. Yet this is no cause for shame, because I know whom I have believed, and am convinced that He is able to guard what I have entrusted to Him until that day. What you heard from me, keep as the pattern of sound teaching, with faith and love in Christ Jesus. Guard the good deposit that was entrusted to you—guard it with the help of the Holy Spirit who lives in us.

—2 Timothy 1:12–14 (NIV)

Paul was in prison and physically in chains when writing this letter to Timothy, a young follower of Christ. Paul knew that his time was about up here on earth. In the verse above, it sounds like he is handing over to Timothy the reins of the responsibility of carrying the gospel of Jesus.

We may not ever be put in physical chains for being a follower of Christ, but daily we are "chained" by the thoughts and opinions that worldly people have about what we believe. We are made to feel ashamed, intolerant, or whatever the world tries to tell us we are because we believe in Christ and His written Word. But be encouraged by Paul, who reminds us that there is no need for us to be ashamed, because we believe in the One who is able to do *all* that He has said He is going to do. Until that day when He returns in all His undeniable glory, you have been given the Holy Spirit to guide and direct you so that you can walk in faith and live in love like Christ teaches us in His Word. Be encouraged and walk with Him! Be blessed!

When he had finished washing their feet, he put on his clothes and returned to his place. "Do you understand what I have done for you?" he asked them. "You call me 'Teacher' and 'Lord,' and rightly so, for that is what I am. Now that I, your Lord and Teacher, have washed your feet, you also should wash one another's feet. I have set you an example that you should do as I have done for you. Very truly I tell you, no servant is greater than his master, nor is a messenger greater than the one who sent him. Now that you know these things, you will be blessed if you do them."

—John 13:12–17 (NIV)

Jesus said this after He had taken the time to wash each disciple's feet (remember that they wore sandals back then, so their feet were not the cleanest). When Jesus came to Peter, Peter felt kind of like, "Lord, what are you doing? You are above this sort of action." With patience Jesus explained, "You don't understand my actions now, but soon you will." With His crucifixion nearly at hand, Jesus was showing the disciples what the cross was going to do for them, namely, cleanse them from their sin. But Jesus also used this as an opportunity to teach His disciples one of the ways they were to proclaim His message of salvation to the world. He told them that even the One they called Master, Teacher, and Lord was willing to serve the servant if the heavenly Father so willed.

Walk with Him! Be blessed!

Herald and preach the Word! Keep your sense of urgency [stand by, be at hand and ready], whether the opportunity seems to be favorable or unfavorable. [Whether it is convenient or inconvenient, whether it is welcome or unwelcome, you as preacher of the Word are to show people in what way their lives are wrong.] And convince them, rebuking and correcting, warning and urging and encouraging them, being unflagging and inexhaustible in patience and teaching.

—2 Timothy 4:2 (AB)

There are lots of instructions in this one little verse. It says to be urgent in sharing God's Word as if someone's life depended on it (and it does), and to do it when it feels comfortable or uncomfortable. Then it moves from speaking to showing. I don't think this means that we are to show people a list of what they are doing wrong and what we are doing right. I think it means that we, as followers of Christ, live out our faith in such a manner that our actions and words are one. This makes it so that those we are wanting to impact are encouraged and not discouraged; they are given hope, not despair. They begin to walk in victory, not in defeat, and they come to Christ through His Word, which has consistently been shared by those who live, breathe, and speak it.

Walk with Him! Be blessed!

No one stood by me the first time I defended myself; all deserted me. May God not count it against them! But the Lord stayed with me and gave me strength, so that I was able to proclaim the full message for all the Gentiles to hear; and I was rescued from being sentenced to death.

—2 Timothy 4:16–17 (GNT)

I have read these verses many times. Each time, I've thought, *Okay, Paul's friends deserted him. Then he went to trial and was let go?* And I have actually thought/wondered why all these little details about Paul's life, and many details about the lives of other people in the Bible, are included in Scripture. Consider this: maybe these details are included so we can relate God's Word to our own daily lives. Many times we experience the same things the people of the Bible experienced, such as loneliness, betrayal, sadness, anger, and hurt. Paul essentially says in these verses, "It is Christ who is there for me. When I stood on trial and no one else was there, my strength was found in Christ. And because of Christ, I can look past the shortcomings of all those who weren't there for me, I won't hold it against them because Christ is enough."

Walk with Him! Be blessed!

Therefore, if you are offering your gift at the altar and there remember that your brother or sister has something against you, leave your gift there in front of the altar. First go and be reconciled to them; then come and offer your gift.

—Matthew 5:23–24 (NIV)

I have had to apologize a lot in my lifetime because I have offended a lot of people, but honestly most of the times when I "apologized" to someone it really wasn't an apology; it was more of a justification as to why I had acted offensively. Even more, what started as an apology ended up with me pointing out to the person how he or she had contributed to my offensive behavior. Usually I sound something like this: "Hey, friend, I am so sorry for such-and-such, but when you did such-and-such, I just such-and-such." (You have the liberty to fill in the instances of "such-and-such" with your own such-and-suches.) But in Scripture it tells us to be reconciled to the other when we have offended someone. It doesn't mention anything about getting an apology back the moment after you ask for forgiveness from someone. I think the verse above is reminding us that our apology should be sincere. "I am so sorry for [whatever it is you are sorry for]. I know I was wrong. I am asking you to forgive me." Once we account for our own actions and ask forgiveness from another, we can go back to Christ and truly experience the forgiveness He died for us to have.

Walk with Him! Be blessed!

The true light that gives light to everyone was coming into the world. He was in the world, and though the world was made through him, the world did not recognize him. He came to that which was his own, but his own did not receive him.

—John 1:9–11 (NIV)

I find it very interesting that after everything Jesus did that fulfilled the very Scriptures the people of His time on earth knew so well, many of those people still did not see Him for who He was. I mean, right in front of them was the Savior of the World, the one they had been looking for and expecting to come was, yet they didn't recognize Him. How could this be? Maybe because Jesus didn't look the part. He didn't appear as they had expected someone of greatness to appear, so much so that when He was right in front of them, living, breathing, walking, talking, and doing miracle after miracle, their own perception of what the Savior should look like and how He should act got in the way. Wow! How many times do we do this same thing to the people around us? Because someone doesn't fit the role, or because someone doesn't match our perception of what a person of his or her ilk should be like, we totally miss someone right in front of us. It is interesting, sad, and very possible that we ourselves would not recognize the Savior.

Walk with Him! Be blessed!

And one of them struck the servant of the high priest, cutting off his right ear. But Jesus answered, "No more of this!" And he touched the man's ear and healed him.

—Luke 22:50–51 (NIV)

Jason Gray performs a song with the lyrics, "Jesus is speaking, but it is so hard to hear when disciples with swords are cutting off ears,"[2] which I am thinking is probably referencing the verses above. In his zeal to defend the gospel, the disciple Peter was showing what lengths he would go to in order to defend Jesus. Yet Jesus told him to back down. Then He restored the ear of the high priest's servant who had been wanting to cause Him harm. Hmm. How many times in our zeal to share the gospel is the effect like cutting off someone's "hearing" of the gospel? Or worse yet, we sometimes decide who should get to hear the gospel because of our view of them.

Evidently Jesus wanted the high priest's servant, who was a part of the group coming to arrest Him, to be able to hear. Christ restored the man's hearing so that he would be able not only to see but also to hear all of what was happening while He was being taken to Pontius Pilate for judgment.

We are not called to decide who hears the gospel of Christ; we are called to speak, live, and love the gospel of Christ in such a way that no one's ears get cut off.

Walk with Him! Be blessed!

---

[2] "Without Running Away," Jason Gray, *A Way to See In the Dark*. EMI Gospel, Centricity Music, compact disc

I have told you these things, so that in me you may have peace. In this world you will have trouble. But take heart! I have overcome the world.

—John 16:33 (NIV)

There are two promises in this verse: (1) We will have struggles in life; (2) Christ has overcome those struggles. When I am experiencing trials, my natural response is, "Okay, God, what am I supposed to learn from this?" I keep God pretty busy, ha-ha, doing whatever needs to be done to bring me into a closer walk with Him. But if I only see my trials as things that benefit me, then I am being very selfish in my thinking of how God works. I mean, just maybe He is saying, "Hey, girl, I need you to bear this burden for a while so ol' so-and-so can see Me working through you. Are you willing to struggle for a while so someone else can see My divine love? Yeah, I know it will be tough and unpleasant, but I promise never to leave you or forsake you. And I will bring you through this difficult time in such a way that you'll move even closer to Me. And the coolest part is that ol' so-and-so is going to want to know My Son because of the hope in Him you are holding onto. And remember He has already overcome this world. I know you know that, but I would like so-and-so to know it as well." So maybe not all trials are about God doing a work in us. Maybe they are about Him doing a work through us.

Walk with Him! Be blessed!

Be strong and courageous, because you will lead these people to inherit the land I swore to their ancestors to give them. Be strong and very courageous. Be careful to obey all the law my servant Moses gave you; do not turn from it to the right or to the left, that you may be successful wherever you go. ... Have I not commanded you? Be strong and courageous. Do not be afraid; do not be discouraged, for the Lord your God will be with you wherever you go. ... Whoever rebels against your word and does not obey it, whatever you may command them, will be put to death. Only be strong and courageous!

—Joshua 1:6–7, 9, 18 (NIV)

I am thinking that God wanted Joshua to be strong and courageous, aren't you? In this chapter, in four out of the eighteen verses, Joshua is encouraged to be strong and courageous. The first time is right after Joshua became the leader (after Moses had died). God said to Joshua, "Now it is you who leads." God mentioned the territory Joshua would be leading the Israelites into, and then He promised, "No one will stand against you all the days of your life. And just like Moses, I will be with you. Now be strong and courageous!" The second time God tells Joshua to be strong and courageous is after God reminded him to follow all the instructions (the law), not turning to the right or to the left (i.e., not getting distracted) so that he would be successful. God encouraged Joshua to keep the book of the law (the Word of God) always on his lips, meditating on it day and night. The third time God tells Joshua to be strong and courageous is after God simply said, "Have I not commanded you?" He essentially said, "I believe in you, Joshua. You can do what I have asked you to do. You believe in Me, and I will be with you." The last time Joshua is told to be strong and courageous, it is said by the Israelites. After Joshua had told them how they were going to enter the Promised Land, their response was, "Just like we followed Moses, we will follow you, Joshua. God was with Moses, so we have faith that He will be with you. Whatever you say, we will do." They too were encouraging Joshua to be strong and courageous. Evidently Joshua needed some encouragement for what lay ahead. So don't be discouraged when God asks you to follow Him and you don't think you can do it or that it is too much. Just know that He is encouraging you to "be strong and courageous." Just like someone who has walked with God through the wilderness for forty years, we all need to be encouraged to continue on and be strong and courageous. Just continue walking with Him! Be blessed!

And why do you worry about clothes? See how the flowers of the field grow. They do not labor or spin. Yet I tell you that not even Solomon in all his splendor was dressed like one of these. If that is how God clothes the grass of the field, which is here today and tomorrow is thrown into the fire, will he not much more clothe you—you of little faith? So do not worry, saying, "What shall we eat?" or "What shall we drink?" or "What shall we wear?" For the pagans run after all these things, and your heavenly Father knows that you need them. But seek first his kingdom and his righteousness, and all these things will be given to you as well. Therefore do not worry about tomorrow, for tomorrow will worry about itself. Each day has enough trouble of its own.

—Matthew 6:28–34 (NIV)

One November, things were put into place in such a way that caused my husband, Ted, and me to have a different plan from the one to which we had become accustomed. During this time, many different options were presented to us. One day we would say, "Well, today it appears we will...," and then the next day it would be, "Well, today it appears we will ..." This pattern went on for about four months and was almost comical. It was such an interesting time to be totally at the mercy of God. We literally had no clue about what to do except to wait until we were given the go-ahead to move. And move we did—to Montana! Even then it was a waiting game, as I had spent the summer in Missouri and had just arrived in Montana. During that time it was still, "Well, today ..." Now that I am in Montana and it appears that Ted and I have direction for our tomorrows, the struggle isn't in adjusting to being miles away from family and friends and life as we have known it but in going back to taking our tomorrows into our own hands and not walking in the promises of the verse above. God knows what we need for today. He just wants us to seek Him. He's got the rest. So today I will seek Him and walk with Him.

Be blessed!

And many came to him. And they said, "John did no sign, but everything that John said about this man was true." And many believed in him there.

—John 10:41–42 (ESV)

In the above verse, people are talking about Jesus. John the Baptist is the one giving them something to talk about. John had been declaring that Jesus was coming. After Jesus was baptized, John started declaring, "Jesus is here." And the people to whom John spoke then had the privilege of seeing his words come to be true. Everything he had been saying about Jesus was true. They saw it in the way Jesus spoke, the way He lived, and the way He glorified God, His purpose for being here. And many believed. John didn't do miracles; he just spoke the truth about Jesus—and then Jesus lived the truth. Do you realize that we, just like John, have the privilege of speaking the truth about Jesus? Even more than that, we have the privilege of living the truth just like Jesus did so that many will believe. Walk with Him! Be blessed!

God wants you to silence stupid and ignorant people by doing right. You are free, but still you are God's servants, and you must not use your freedom as an excuse for doing wrong.

—1 Peter 2:15–16 (CEV)

Do you remember having a newfound freedom after you accepted Christ as your Lord and Savior? The burdens of life were lifted away and truly there was a newness to life. "We were buried therefore with him through baptism unto death: that like as Christ was raised from the dead through the glory of the Father, so we also might walk in newness of life" (Romans 6:4 ASV). This is very similar to the Israelites leaving Egypt. Can you imagine their thoughts after four hundred years of living in bondage and finally being set free? Unfortunately we are too much like the Israelites with our newfound freedom. Too often we start grumbling, questioning, and acting just like they did when we find that the journey is a little longer than we may like; when more is asked of us than we were expecting; and when we forget what we have been set free from (the burden of sin). Maybe this is because we don't fully get the why of our new freedom. The Israelites were brought out of bondage in Egypt not only to be set free from slavery but also, even more important, for God to be glorified and to show the other nations that God is the one true God. This is just like your salvation. Yes, you are saved for eternity, but you are also saved so that Jesus will be glorified and be known as God's Son. It isn't about us or them (the Israelites); it is about God and God's Son. We are saved not just to be set free but also to glorify Christ.

Walk with Him! Be blessed!

May these words of my mouth and this meditation of my heart
be pleasing in your sight, Lord, my Rock and my Redeemer.

—Psalms 19:14 (NIV)

While I was watching NCAA football one day, one commentator said
something like, "Is Johnny Football's only real mistake that he isn't Tim
Tebow?" And then the commentator said something in reference to how
Tim Tebow lives, saying that it isn't really doable for 99.9 percent of us.
My take on that comment is that whether we are living to please self or to
please God, we are going to be criticized and questioned by other people.
If we live to please self, then the world is appalled. If we live for Christ,
then the world thinks we are trying to live unrealistically. Actually the
world wants us to live to meet its way of living and thinking, which keeps
changing. But God desires us to have hearts and minds that are pleasing
and acceptable to Him, our Rock and Redeemer. The world sends us
mixed messages about what it wants and expects from us, but Jesus is very
clear: "He answered, 'Love the Lord your God with all your heart and with
all your soul and with all your strength and with all your mind'; and, 'Love
your neighbor as yourself'" (Luke 10:27 NIV). Be prepared to be criticized
as you walk with Him.

Be blessed!

And my God will meet all your needs according to the riches of his glory in Christ Jesus.

—Philippians 4:19 (NIV)

This verse on its own may not sound very impactful, but know that it is found at the end of the letter Paul wrote to the Philippians. When you read the whole book of Philippians, you see that it expresses the bringing together of everything Paul is encouraging, instructing, and reminding and the Philippians to do. He is saying, "You have done a lot for the call of Christ on your life, but you aren't done. You have more to do. You have blessed me, but you are not done blessing people. You have more to bless. You have learned a lot about Christ and His truth, but you aren't done learning about Christ. You have more to learn. Now go and do it, and remember that you will be able to do all of this because my God not only is going to meet you right where you are for everything that is ahead but also He already has given you everything you need because of His glory, which comes from His Son's righteousness. You already have what you need to do what is ahead. Go with confidence. Through Christ's righteousness, you will be able to see God's glory."

Walk with Him! Be blessed!

> Keep on asking, and you will receive what you ask for. Keep on seeking, and you will find. Keep on knocking, and the door will be opened to you.

—Matthew 7:7 (NLT)

I love how this verse encourages us always to expect an answer from God. It tells us to keep asking and then says that we will receive. Keep seeking and we will find. Keep knocking and the door will open. The kicker is that we have gotten so good at asking, seeking, and knocking that we are missing the answers, the results, and the open doors. This is because what we have to say to God has become more important to us than what God has to say. What we are seeking has become more important to us than what God has to show us. The door we want opened is more important to us than the door God wants to open for us.

Has what you have to say to God become more important than what God has to say to you? This is a tough question, but it is one that I need to ask myself daily.

Walk with Him! Be blessed!

Then God said, "You've been going around in circles in these hills long enough; go north. Command the people, "You're about to cut through the land belonging to your relatives, the People of Esau who settled in Seir. They are terrified of you, but restrain yourselves. Don't try and start a fight. I am not giving you so much as a square inch of their land. I've already given all the hill country of Seir to Esau—he owns it all. Pay them up front for any food or water you get from them." God, your God, has blessed you in everything you have done. He has guarded you in your travels through this immense wilderness. For forty years now, God, your God, has been right here with you. You haven't lacked one thing. So we detoured around our brothers, the People of Esau who live in Seir, avoiding the Arabah Road that comes up from Elath and Ezion Geber; instead we used the road through the Wilderness of Moab. God told me, "And don't try to pick a fight with the Moabites. I am not giving you any of their land. I've given ownership of Ar to the People of Lot." ... God said, "It's time now to cross the Brook Zered." So we crossed the Brook Zered. ... God said to me, "This is the day you cut across the territory of Moab, at Ar. When you approach the People of Ammon, don't try and pick a fight with them because I'm not giving you any of the land of the People of Ammon for yourselves—I've already given it to the People of Lot. On your feet now. Get started. Cross the Brook Arnon. Look: Here's Sihon the Amorite king of Heshbon and his land. I'm handing it over to you—it's all yours. Go ahead, take it. Go to war with him. Before the day is out, I'll make sure that all the people around here are thoroughly terrified. Rumors of you are going to spread like wildfire; they'll totally panic."

—Deuteronomy 2:2–9, 13, 16–25 (MSG)

Here God is walking through the wilderness (aka life) with the Israelites, who are about to be allowed to enter into the Promised Land. Remember they had been wandering for forty years. Their journey in actuality was much shorter, but it took them that long to become ready to really follow God's words and instructions. And now He was about to give them some really important ones. Three times God took the Israelites past or through lands that He had already given to someone else (the people of Esau, the Moabites, and Lot), and He gave very clear instructions: "These people are scared to death of you, but do not harm them. As a matter of fact, pay them for what they provide you. And then keep moving, because I am taking you to your own Promised Land." Then when the Israelites got to where He was taking them, He said, "Now go in and take your land. I have made these people very afraid of you. They have already heard how I, your God, have provided for you throughout this journey. They are going to panic."

Here are some things to consider: (1) God knows when we are really ready to listen to and follow His guidance for our life. If the Israelites had been allowed to go through this last part of their journey any earlier, they might not have listened to God telling them to keep going because what He had provided for the clan of Esau, the Moabites, and Lot might have looked so tempting that they might have heard His instructions but been unwilling to follow them. God knows our hearts; that is how His timing is perfect. He knows when we are *really* willing to follow Him. (2) Never once while allowing the Israelites to see how He had provided for others did God say, "Hold on. What I have for you is better than what I have for them." He did say, "Keep going, because this isn't what I have for you. This is what I have provided for them." We tend to think that if God gives something to someone else, not to us, then He is saving something *better* for us. Hmm, maybe in these Scriptures we can see that God gives differently to people because what He gives is always His best.

Walk with Him! Be blessed!

In the beginning God created the heavens and the earth. Now the earth was formless and empty, darkness was over the surface of the deep, and the Spirit of God was hovering over the waters. And God said, "Let there be light," and there was light. God saw that the light was good, and he separated the light from the darkness. God called the light "day," and the darkness he called "night." And there was evening, and there was morning—the first day. And God said, "Let there be a vault between the waters to separate water from water." So God made the vault and separated the water under the vault from the water above it. And it was so. God called the vault "sky." And there was evening, and there was morning— the second day. And God said, "Let the water under the sky be gathered to one place, and let dry ground appear." And it was so. God called the dry ground "land," and the gathered waters he called "seas." And God saw that it was good. Then God said, "Let the land produce vegetation: seed-bearing plants and trees on the land that bear fruit with seed in it, according to their various kinds." And it was so. The land produced vegetation: plants bearing seed according to their kinds and trees bearing fruit with seed in it according to their kinds. And God saw that it was good. And there was evening, and there was morning—the third day.

—Genesis 1:1–13 (NIV)

Going through Glacier National Park and seeing the splendid display of God's almighty breath and hand only made these verses seem even more true to me. There was nothing about that place that denied Him, the Creator. Everything is so perfectly placed and continually changing that only the One who created it could continue to maintain it. Pictures don't do the park justice. Only when you are there do you begin to understand the magnitude of God's design. When I was at Glacier National Park, it truly was a moment of being in the presence of God in a totally different way than I had ever experienced.

Walk with Him! Be blessed!

After saying these things, he said to them, "Our friend Lazarus has fallen asleep, but I go to awaken him." The disciples said to him, "Lord, if he has fallen asleep, he will recover." Now Jesus had spoken of his death, but they thought that he meant taking rest in sleep. Then Jesus told them plainly, "Lazarus has died, and for your sake I am glad that I was not there, so that you may believe. But let us go to him."

—John 11:11–15 (ESV)

So Thomas, called the Twin, said to his fellow disciples, "Let us also go, that we may die with him."

—John 11:16 (ESV)

What follows is a perfect example of how sometimes when Jesus speaks to us, our own thoughts and perceptions keep us from hearing what He is saying.

Jesus: I am going to go wake Lazarus.

Disciples: He is fine. He is just sleeping. Don't waste Your time. You have more important things to do.

Jesus: Let Me clarify: Lazarus has died. And so that you have the opportunity to believe in Me even more, we will go to Lazarus.

Disciples: Oh, but Jesus, we are going back to where they were trying to kill You. But, okay, we will go so we can die too.

The foregoing must have been one of those just-smile-and-nod moments for Jesus. Man, I wonder how many of those I have given Christ in my life.

Walk with Him! Be blessed!

Honor your father and your mother, so that you may live long in the land the Lord your God is giving you.

—Exodus 20:12 (NIV)

I love how this verse has spoken to me in different ways because of where I was in life when I heard or read it. When I was a child, it pretty much meant, "Do what your parents ask you to do." When I was a teenager, it was more like, "Do what your parents tell you to do or else." When I became a young parent, it meant, "Tell me what to do, please!" As my children became young adults, it became, "Wow! Tell me, Mom and Dad: how did you love me enough to let me go?" When I had the privilege of caring for my parents when they were aging, it was, "Let me show you by my love the way you have loved and cared for me." Now that they both are in heaven with Jesus, it is, "Thank you again and again for teaching me about Him. And because of that, I will see you again." The thing I see as I write this is that it was me who changed as time passed, not my parents' love. Similarly, Christ's love for us is always the same; it never changes. But our understanding of His love only comes as we grow up in Him.

Walk with Him! Be blessed!

> Now when Mary came to where Jesus was and saw him, she fell at his feet, saying to him, "Lord, if you had been here, my brother would not have died." When Jesus saw her weeping, and the Jews who had come with her also weeping, he was deeply moved in his spirit and greatly troubled. And he said, "Where have you laid him?" They said to him, "Lord, come and see." ... So the Jews said, "See how he loved him!" But some of them said, "Could not he who opened the eyes of the blind man also have kept this man from dying?"

> —John 11:32–34, 36–37 (ESV)

Once again, Jesus is speaking, living, and taking action right before people, yet they still don't have the eyes to see Him for who He actually is.

Mary: Jesus, if You had been where You were supposed to be, then this wouldn't have happened.

The Jews: If He were who He says He is, then this guy wouldn't have died in the first place.

We tend to see Christ from such a human perspective that what we expect from Him gets in the way of our seeing Him for who He is. If we could keep this verse in mind—"For my thoughts are not your thoughts, neither are your ways my ways, declares the Lord" (Isaiah 55:8 ESV)—when seeking the Lord, it would probably help us to understand who He is and how He works.

Walk with Him! Be blessed!

By faith Moses, when he was born, was hid three months of his parents, because they saw he was a proper child; and they were not afraid of the king's commandment.

—Hebrews 11:23 (KJV)

One day I was reading Hebrews 11, which starts with, "Now faith is the substance of things hoped for, the evidence of things not seen" (Hebrews 11:1 KJV), and then continues on with many examples of people choosing to have faith in the promises of God that are found throughout His Word. On that particular day, verse 23 really jumped out at me. Moses's parents chose to believe God (have faith) over fearing the authority of human beings over their lives. The king had issued the command to kill any male child born. Instead of doing this, Moses's parents believed God and risked it all, hiding their infant son Moses for three months and then putting him in a basket and floating him down a river, where he would be found by Pharaoh's own daughter, who would take him to the palace to be raised in the very place from which the command that he be killed had been issued. Man, Moses's parents definitely had faith in things not seen but hoped for. I am not sure that they foresaw that Moses would be the deliverer of God's people. They just had more faith and hope in God than they had a fear of humankind.

Walk with Him! Be blessed!

Then Jesus, deeply moved again, came to the tomb. It was a cave, and a stone lay against it. Jesus said, "Take away the stone." Martha, the sister of the dead man, said to him, "Lord, by this time there will be an odor, for he has been dead four days." Jesus said to her, "Did I not tell you that if you believed you would see the glory of God?"

—John 11:38–40 (ESV)

Unfortunately all too many times I sound like Martha. I ask Christ for directions, and when it becomes apparent He is about to do something, whether grand or small, I still think I have to make sure that He knows what He is doing. I love how He very patiently reminds Martha (i.e., me), "Didn't I tell you that you would see God's glory?" In the verses above, Lazarus was being brought back to life not only because his sisters were saddened by his loss but also, and even more important, so that God would be glorified.

When God moves in our lives, it is to meet a need we have at that moment or in a moment to come, but we must not miss the fact that He moves to be glorified. Christ died to give us eternal life, but even more than that He died for God the Father to be glorified. Let us not forget that it isn't all about us; it is more about Him. The designer, the Creator, and the giver of life came to die in order to be glorified. Walk with Him! Be blessed!

As you enter the home, give it your greeting. If the home is deserving, let your peace rest on it; if it is not, let your peace return to you. If anyone will not welcome you or listen to your words, leave that home or town and shake the dust off your feet.

—Matthew 10:12–14 (NIV)

Jesus gave these instructions to the disciples as He was sending them out to share the good news of Him. We are sent out to share Christ today, although most of us are called to share not by traveling from town to town but by traveling through the relationships in our lives. So is it possible that we too should sometimes leave a relationship and shake the dust off our feet? The verses above do not give us a time table or tell us how long we are to invest in a relationship, but there could come a time when we are no longer called to stay. Jesus told the disciples this before they even left Him to begin traveling on their own, so we shouldn't be surprised if He tells us that it is time to leave when we are in the midst of a relationship. We must be prepared to go if called to do so. And not only that, we must dust off our feet when we do leave. Now I know that the dusting off of the feet was symbolic, a sign that the work there was done and the disciples should no longer take responsibility for the people in that home or town (compare this to Pontius Pilate washing his hands at Jesus's trial), but I think it isn't a symbol just to the people who are being left. It is a symbol to us as well. When we are called to leave, we must really be willing to let go, and to trust God for what happens next, not just to us but also to the people we are moved away from. Notice too that Jesus never told the disciples to stop praying for those people. He just told them to be prepared to leave when the time came. Leaving might just enable you to see God work not only in the other people's lives but also in yours, which would be better than staying anyway.

Walk with Him! Be blessed!

Jesus answered, "It is written: 'Man shall not live on bread alone, but on every word that comes from the mouth of God.'"

—Matthew 4:4 (NIV)

If we fed our physical bodies with food like we feed our souls with the Word of God, then many of us would end up sick and in dire need of immediate attention. Oh, wait, that describes the condition of many. We need to get to God's emergency room! His Word is medicine to our soul. This medicine heals our life, relationships, and spirit. Find the medicine your soul is needing today in the Word of the almighty Creator of the very thing you are living: life. Walk with Him! Be blessed!

So we aren't depressed. But even if our bodies are breaking down on the outside, the person that we are on the inside is being renewed every day. Our temporary minor problems are producing an eternal stockpile of glory for us that is beyond all comparison.

—2 Corinthians 4:16–17 (CEB)

Have you ever had to talk yourself off a ledge, not a literal ledge but what I would call an emotional ledge? The ledge is where your emotions seem to want to run amok, and every time you think you have them in check, they flair back up. On the outside you appear as if everything is hunky-dory, but inside you are a wreck.

Why does this verse talk about your outer being going down the drain while your inner being is getting better? Well, because it reminds us of where the true change in us comes from. The change Christ offers us comes from within. Christ works from within us, making us a new creation. All those emotions that we keep inside that cause havoc in our inner being (which is where Christ is changing us) don't have a hold on us if we let go of them. When we realize we are being renewed from within, our renewal comes from letting go of things like unwieldy emotions that cause us to walk out on those ledges, where we are at greatest risk. We can then look in the mirror and see the physical self perishing but know that the inner self is being renewed, made into the new creation Christ promised we would be made into when we came to Him and accepted His saving grace.

Walk with Him! Be blessed!

John replied, "No one can receive anything unless God gives it from heaven. You yourselves know how plainly I told you, 'I am not the Messiah. I am only here to prepare the way for him.' It is the bridegroom who marries the bride, and the best man is simply glad to stand with him and hear his vows. Therefore, I am filled with joy at his success. He must become greater and greater, and I must become less and less. He has come from above and is greater than anyone else. We are of the earth, and we speak of earthly things, but he has come from heaven and is greater than anyone else."

—John 3:27–31 (NLT)

Talk about knowing who you are in Christ. Man, John the Baptist sure did! His followers came to him saying, "Jesus is drawing a bigger crowd than you [us]. That isn't right! We were here first!" Well, maybe they didn't say that. Maybe that is what I would have been saying had I been part of John's crowd, although I wish I could say that such wouldn't have been the case. I can't say that, though; I know myself all too well. Still, I love how John reminds his people that they (we) aren't who they are spreading the news about. "I told you I wasn't the One. I only point to the One. Just like you, just like everyone, we aren't pointing to ourselves but to Jesus." Like John, if our lives aren't becoming less and less about us and more and more about Christ, then we are living in vain. Ask yourself this: if people couldn't remember your name but, because of you, they did know Christ, would you be okay with that?

Walk with Him! Be blessed!

"Joshua, no one will be able to stand up against you as long as you live. I will be with you, just as I was with Moses. I will never leave you. I will never desert you."

—Joshua 1:5 (NIRV)

Do you ever feel like life is spinning out of control and you have totally lost any control you might have had? Do you feel as if the craziness the world presents to you daily is controlling and tossing you about like a leaf on the gales of life? Do you feel that you have totally lost hope of possibly managing your life? If so, then congratulations; you have now reached the point of totally letting go of any hope you bring to life and are now ready to take hold of the only One who holds the "control" you are looking for, the One who bled and died to give you the hope you are looking for, the One who promised never to leave you or forsake you, as He holds not only your yesterdays and tomorrows but also your todays. Let go of the control in which you are trying to find peace and comfort, and take hold of Christ, who has already walked in your today. Let Him guide you through. Let go, and let God do what only He plans on doing. Walk with Him! Be blessed!

As evening came, Jesus said to his disciples, "Let's cross to the other side of the lake." So they took Jesus in the boat and started out, leaving the crowds behind (although other boats followed). But soon a fierce storm came up. High waves were breaking into the boat, and it began to fill with water. Jesus was sleeping at the back of the boat with his head on a cushion. The disciples woke him up, shouting, "Teacher, don't you care that we're going to drown?" When Jesus woke up, he rebuked the wind and said to the waves, "Silence! Be still!" Suddenly the wind stopped, and there was a great calm. Then he asked them, "Why are you afraid? Do you still have no faith?" The disciples were absolutely terrified. "Who is this man?" they asked each other. "Even the wind and waves obey him!"

—Mark 4:35–41 (NLT)

Jesus speaks to us and says, "Come on with Me, over here." We jump in the boat and go. Yet the ride ends up being different from what we had expected. The waters get rough, the waves are high, and fear sets in. Then comes doubt. "Maybe I misunderstood the directions. Maybe He meant that I should come in the morning, when I could actually see the other side, or to wait until the storm season was over to cross the sea. Because it wouldn't be scary or dangerous if I had heard correctly, right?" Or maybe these thoughts come to be: "Jesus, what were You thinking by having me get in the boat when You knew a storm was coming? You supposedly know everything, so why did You allow me to get overtaken by this storm when You very well could have prevented it?" This makes us very much like the disciples, who got to walk physically with Jesus for three years, in that we tend to question who He really is; we tend to think He doesn't really care what is going on in our lives; and we tend to be shocked when find ourselves safe on dry land. Thank you, Lord, for your patience with me as I learn, just like the disciples did, to walk with You.

Be blessed!

These are the commands, decrees, and regulations that the Lord your God commanded me to teach you. You must obey them in the land you are about to enter and occupy, and you and your children and grandchildren must fear the Lord your God as long as you live. If you obey all his decrees and commands, you will enjoy a long life. Listen closely, Israel, and be careful to obey. Then all will go well with you, and you will have many children in the land flowing with milk and honey, just as the Lord, the God of your ancestors, promised you. Listen, O Israel! The Lord is our God, the Lord alone. And you must love the Lord your God with all your heart, all your soul, and all your strength. And you must commit yourselves wholeheartedly to these commands that I am giving you today. Repeat them again and again to your children. Talk about them when you are at home and when you are on the road, when you are going to bed and when you are getting up. Tie them to your hands and wear them on your forehead as reminders. Write them on the doorposts of your house and on your gates.

—Deuteronomy 6:1–9 (NLT)

The verses above express the last instructions Moses gave to the Israelites before sending them into the Promised Land. It is made pretty clear that the Promised Land wouldn't be the Promised Land if the Israelites didn't keep God first, but it is also made clear that the family (parents) are to be the teachers of the children, teaching them about the promises of God. From these verses of Deuteronomy, I discern that we are to love the Lord our God with all our heart, all our soul, and all our strength. We are to write it all over the place, on the fences, on the doorpost, on our hands, on our forehead. We are to talk about it when we lie down, when we get up, when we are home, and when we are on the road. And if we do this, then we will live well.

Who is teaching your children about our Lord and Savior? The world? Your culture? MTV? Disney? Or is it the home? Which voice do they hear more? Do we, like many businesses do, outsource our children to things of this world to be taught about Jesus?

Walk with Him! Be blessed!

Then, going over to the people who sold doves, he told them, "Get these things out of here. Stop turning my Father's house into a marketplace!" Then his disciples remembered this prophecy from the Scriptures: "Passion for God's house will consume me." But the Jewish leaders demanded, "What are you doing? If God gave you authority to do this, show us a miraculous sign to prove it." "All right," Jesus replied. "Destroy this temple, and in three days I will raise it up." "What!" they exclaimed. "It has taken forty-six years to build this Temple, and you can rebuild it in three days?" But when Jesus said "this temple," he meant his own body.

—John 2:16–21 (NLT)

Wow! Jesus was not a meek person as we tend to view Him many times. He just knew when to take a stand and when to respond quietly. Unfortunately, we let our human perspective of Christ get in our way all too often. We view Him as a human, which He was, and forget He is also God. Maybe if we could remember that He is God, our awe and wonder of who He is wouldn't waver like it does.

Walk with Him! Be blessed!

My dear brothers and sisters, stand firm. Don't let anything move you. Always give yourselves completely to the work of the Lord. Because you belong to the Lord, you know that your work is not worthless.

—1 Corinthians 15:58 (NIRV)

In today's changing world, where people are seeking the next great idea, the verse above is a reminder that we have been given something to stand on that has not changed since the beginning of time: God's loving plan for us, both for humankind as a whole and for us as individuals. Life was breathed into Adam to begin the first relationship between God and man. Adam was given the "job" of caring for the garden of Eden, and God promised to walk with him. Adam (and Eve) stumbled on the job (didn't stand firm on his promise), so the Father sent the Son to make right what humankind had damaged, the relationship between God and human beings. Now through Christ we are to continue standing firm on what the Father began.

Just like Adam, we have a "job." Our job is to share Christ. Just like Adam was instructed to care for the garden, we are instructed to care for the message of Christ and not waver in the truth of Christ. The truth of Christ while we are sharing Christ is not to be changed. We are to stand firm, not stumbling or being moved by this world. God's love through Christ is the *one* constant in this world and has been since the beginning. Share, stand firm, don't be moved, and walk with Him. Be blessed!

When Jesus had tasted it, he said, "It is finished!" Then he bowed his head and released his spirit.

—John 19:30 (NLT)

And as they went, Jesus met them and greeted them. And they ran to him, grasped his feet, and worshiped him. Then Jesus said to them, "Don't be afraid! Go tell my brothers to leave for Galilee, and they will see me there."

—Matthew 28:9–10 (NLT)

The phrase *defining moment* has become very popular in our culture today. Whether it is being used in sports to mean that someone has achieved some level through one moment that has finally identified what kind of athlete he or she is or isn't; in life when a person has finally received clarity upon which he or she can base the rest of his or her life; or to describe an aha moment that shows what kind of person someone is, setting that person on a path to follow for the rest of his or her days; *defining moment* has become a common phrase. Understandably we all want something to help us make sense, or more sense, of this thing called life. We think that if we could just understand or explain things more, then we could better predict what is to come. If someone has been defined as a certain kind of athlete, we know what to expect from him. When he doesn't continue to live up to that definition, we have the right to be disappointed and critical. When we experience our aha moment, we know what to expect from life because our level of understanding has been expanded and, well, we just get it, right? Well, my aha, or defining, moment came when I realized there are really only three defining moments in life: (1) Christ's virgin birth; (2) Christ's death on the cross (He alone lived His life to be the perfect sacrifice to atone for the sins of the world); and (3) Christ's resurrection (He alone overcame death, which was the penalty for the sins of the world). My acceptance of all three of His defining moments by faith is what I need to define this thing called life.

Walk with Him! Be blessed!

But there is a great difference between Adam's sin and God's gracious gift. For the sin of this one man, Adam, brought death to many. But even greater is God's wonderful grace and his gift God's free gift leads to our being made right with God, even though we are guilty of many of forgiveness to many through this other man, Jesus Christ. And the result of God's gracious gift is very different from the result of that one man's sin. For Adam's sin led to condemnation, but sins. For the sin of this one man, Adam, caused death to rule over many. But even greater is God's wonderful grace and his gift of righteousness, for all who receive it will live in triumph over sin and death through this one man, Jesus Christ. Yes, Adam's one sin brings condemnation for everyone, but Christ's one act of righteousness brings a right relationship with God and new life for everyone. Because one person disobeyed God, many became sinners. But because one other person obeyed God, many will be made righteous.

—Romans 5:15–19 (NLT)

The verses above speak of the great contrast between humanity's way and God's way. Humanity's way brings condemnation and destruction, whereas God's way brings righteousness and life. Humanity's way brings separation and isolation, whereas God's way brings fellowship and a walk with Him through Christ. Humanity's way brings loneliness and death, whereas God's way brings peace and renewal by grace. Which side are you allowing to cover your life? People don't like to admit there are sides to be chosen, but there are. Since the time of Christ's birth and resurrection, the line has been drawn. And we are on one side or the other. The amazing thing is that the one side has already won all the battles that have been fought, are being fought, and will be fought. So it comes down to this question: which side of the line are you on?

Walk with Him! Be blessed!

So we do not lose heart. Though our outer self is wasting away, our inner self is being renewed day by day. For this light momentary affliction is preparing for us an eternal weight of glory beyond all comparison, as we look not to the things that are seen but to the things that are unseen. For the things that are seen are transient, but the things that are unseen are eternal.

—2 Corinthians 4:16–1 (ESV)

Our hope is not in this world but in God, who promises never to leave us or forsake us. He alone can heal the pain we feel about the devastation of our yesterdays and todays. Finding our comfort in Christ will allow our eyes to be opened to His eternal love. Walk with Him! Be blessed!

He will bring you to the land that belonged to your people long ago. You will take it over. He'll make you better off than your people were. He'll increase your numbers more than he increased theirs. The Lord your God will keep your hearts from being stubborn. He'll do the same thing for your children and their children. Then you will love him with all your heart and with all your soul. And you will live.

—Deuteronomy 30:5–6 (NIRV)

Imagine if God gave you these instructions today, especially if you had just spent the last forty years traipsing around the wilderness and you were more than ready to saunter into your Promised Land. "Wait! What, Lord? I have to take the land myself? Isn't it enough that I have wandered out here in the wilderness for all these years? Can't I just walk in and have it all be handed to me? Because of my past, don't I deserve something easy to come my way? You expect more from me? When does it ever stop being hard and get to be easy? … What? Oh, You never promised easy, but You did promise to never leave me or forsake me. Read on? … It might not be easy, but I will be better off because I have walked with You. And even more importantly, You have my children's lives in Your care. We are going to come to love You with all our hearts and soul, and then we will know what it means to live. Okay, Lord, here we go!"

Walk with Him! Be blessed!

For God called you to do good, even if it means suffering, just as Christ suffered for you. He is your example, and you must follow in his steps. He never sinned, nor ever deceived anyone. He did not retaliate when he was insulted, nor threaten revenge when he suffered. He left his case in the hands of God, who always judges fairly. He personally carried our sins in his body on the cross so that we can be dead to sin and live for what is right. By his wounds you are healed. Once you were like sheep who wandered away. But now you have turned to your Shepherd, the Guardian of your souls.

—1 Peter 2:21–25 (NLT)

Wow! We all want to do good, but are we willing to suffer in order to do good? Christ is our example, but how often do we follow in His steps? We can't, nor are we called to, be perfect as Christ is, but we are called to defend our beliefs like Christ defended Himself. He let God handle His defense.

The gospel of Jesus can defend itself when we present it the way Christ presented it. We just need to present it the way He presented it. It says in Luke 19:10, "The son of man came to seek and to save that which was lost." But too often my translation comes across as, "Jesus came so I can prove other people wrong and prove that I am right." Focusing on following His example instead of impressing people with what we know is a much better way of following Him.

Walk with Him! Be blessed!

For every kind of beasts and birds, of creeping things and things in the sea, is tamed, and hath been tamed by mankind. But the tongue can no man tame; it is a restless evil, it is full of deadly poison. Therewith bless we the Lord and Father; and therewith curse we men, who are made after the likeness of God: out of the same mouth cometh forth blessing and cursing. My brethren, these things ought not so to be.

—James 3:7–10 (ASV)

In today's world, it seems that something is always being said that offends someone somewhere. And if we go to the Word of God, we find that we should not be surprised by this, because the Word tells us the tongue cannot be tamed. So what is one to do? Like with everything else, we should look to Christ for the answer. When Jesus lived on earth, people did a lot of talking about Him. He could have easily been offended by what they were saying, turned His focus from doing what He was called to do, and spent His time trying to change their opinion. But He didn't. He was so rooted in knowing who He was and what He was here to do that He stayed the course no matter what people were saying about Him. He didn't become distracted by the "offensive" things being said, nor did He become puffed up with pride and full of Himself because of the praise He received. He was so convinced of who He was and what His life was about that He could not be persuaded otherwise by others' thoughts and opinions.

Maybe we need to be more rooted in who we are in Christ so we won't be so quick to be offended by the opinions of others, especially those that differ from our own beliefs. So next time we are offended by the words or opinions of another, instead of remaining offended we should stand on our beliefs and on who we are in Christ. And maybe instead of being offended by what appears to be our opinion, the one who offended us will come to know the saving grace of Christ through the same love shown by our heavenly Father over two thousand years ago when He sent His Son to be the Savior of this world. Christ didn't come to offend; He came to give eternal life, which begins when we accept His gift. Walk with Him! Be blessed!

Most important of all, continue to show deep love for each other, for love covers a multitude of sins. Cheerfully share your home with those who need a meal or a place to stay. God has given each of you a gift from his great variety of spiritual gifts. Use them well to serve one another. Do you have the gift of speaking? Then speak as though God himself were speaking through you. Do you have the gift of helping others? Do it with all the strength and energy that God supplies. Then everything you do will bring glory to God through Jesus Christ. All glory and power to him forever and ever! Amen.

—1 Peter 4:8–11 (NLT)

In one translation of the verses above, the word used in place of *deeply* (which is how we are instructed to love) is *intensely*, which is quite interesting because the latter word actually means "to be stretched or strained." But how willing are we to actually be stretched or strained to love others, especially those who aren't easily loved and when it causes us discomfort? We are asked to love others cheerfully. Only when we live with a humble servant's heart, like Christ Himself lived, can we love intensely like we are called to do. I believe we all want to love others but that many times our heart gets in the way because we haven't yet humbled ourselves before the Lord. Imagine standing at the cross, looking up into His eyes, and knowing that He doesn't deserve to be there but that He is there because of you and your sin. Maybe then your heart will begin to be humbled so that you can love intensely and can serve like He does. Walk with Him! Be blessed!

Dear friends, don't be surprised at the fiery trials you are going through, as if something strange were happening to you. Instead, be very glad—for these trials make you partners with Christ in his suffering, so that you will have the wonderful joy of seeing his glory when it is revealed to all the world. So be happy when you are insulted for being a Christian, for then the glorious Spirit of God rests upon you. If you suffer, however, it must not be for murder, stealing, making trouble, or prying into other people's affairs. But it is no shame to suffer for being a Christian. Praise God for the privilege of being called by his name! For the time has come for judgment, and it must begin with God's household. And if judgment begins with us, what terrible fate awaits those who have never obeyed God's Good News?

—1 Peter 4:12–17 (NLT)

Life is full of trials and struggles (suffering), some of which are blessed by the Lord so as to bring us into a closer relationship with Him. But many of our trials are the result of our own doing, stuff we don't want to own up to. Notice that the above verse reads, "If you suffer it must not be from murder [killing people with one's tongue] stealing [taking credit when it belongs to someone else or Christ] making trouble [being the one that has to have the last word, or only following guidelines when someone is looking] prying into other people's business [thinking we know what is better for someone or trying to control others]." But if we are truly looked down on for following Christ, we should have no shame but see it as an honor. We need to make sure we know the reason for our suffering.

Walk with Him! Be blessed!

As they were walking along the road, a man said to him, "I will follow you wherever you go." Jesus replied, "Foxes have dens and birds have nests, but the Son of Man has no place to lay his head." He said to another man, "Follow me." But he replied, "Lord, first let me go and bury my father." Jesus said to him, "Let the dead bury their own dead, but you go and proclaim the kingdom of God." Still another said, "I will follow you, Lord; but first let me go back and say goodbye to my family." Jesus replied, "No one who puts a hand to the plow and looks back is fit for service in the kingdom of God."

—Luke 9:57–62 (NIV)

How many times in my life have I sounded like all three of the people described in the verses above? "Lord, I want to follow You. Please let me know Your will for my life. And, oh yeah, here are the conditions I need for my will to line up with Yours." If only what I wanted to do and what I know I am supposed to do were always in line with following Christ, my life would be a breeze. Praise the Lord; He is patient with me. In those times when I have given up my "want to" for His "supposed to," He has shown me His faithfulness, and my trust in Him has grown. Hopefully someday my "want to" and "supposed to" will always be the same. I think that this verse says it best: "Delight yourself in the Lord and He will give you the desires of your heart" (Psalms 37:4)!

Walk with Him! Be blessed!

Think back on those early days when you first learned about Christ. Remember how you remained faithful even though it meant terrible suffering. Sometimes you were exposed to public ridicule and were beaten, and sometimes you helped others who were suffering the same things. You suffered along with those who were thrown into jail, and when all you owned was taken from you, you accepted it with joy. You knew there were better things waiting for you that will last forever. So do not throw away this confident trust in the Lord. Remember the great reward it brings you! Patient endurance is what you need now, so that you will continue to do God's will. Then you will receive all that he has promised. "For in just a little while, the Coming One will come and not delay. And my righteous ones will live by faith. But I will take no pleasure in anyone who turns away." But we are not like those who turn away from God to their own destruction. We are the faithful ones, whose souls will be saved.

—Hebrews 10:32–39 (NLT)

Some days we just need to be reminded of why we should get out of bed. We should get out of bed not to make our way through this world for ourselves but so that we may bring glory to the Lord. Our worst days don't compare to His day on the cross and the three days He spent in the grave. Because He did that, we can walk with Him.

Be blessed!

Let us hold tightly without wavering to the hope we affirm, for God can be trusted to keep his promise. Let us think of ways to motivate one another to acts of love and good works. And let us not neglect our meeting together, as some people do, but encourage one another, especially now that the day of his return is drawing near.

—Hebrews 10:23–25 (NLT)

It is always interesting how a new year gives us permission to start anew. We may not have accomplished every task we had wanted to accomplish or completed enough of the things on our list of things to do in the previous year, but the changing over of the calendar seems to make us okay with that because it gives us permission to start a new list of to-dos or of goals to meet. We allow ourselves to let go of the not started, the incomplete, and to wipe the desk clean and start afresh. This is wonderful. We all need new beginnings and need to be refreshed, but this year I want a new ending. So instead of being a little more determined to do better, accomplish a little more, and be more disciplined, I am going to put this verse, Hebrews 10:23–25 (along with the rest of the Word of God), on my list of to-dos. I will do the following things: (1) hold tightly to the hope that comes from the promises of God, as He can be trusted; (2) encourage and motivate others with the same love and encouragement Christ gives me daily through His Word and presence; (3) meet with other believers so that I will be encouraged and motivated through the love they have received from Christ; and (4) expect His presence or His return.

Walk with Him! Be blessed!

But as for me my prayer is to You O Lord at an acceptable
time O God in the abundance of Your steadfast love answer
me in Your saving fullness!

—Psalms 69:13 (ESV)

I love this verse. It speaks so much about the writer, who is saying the
following things: (1) My prayer goes only to You, Lord, knowing that You,
God, are the only one who has the answer. (2) It is in Your perfect timing
that the answer will come, as You are full of saving grace. (3) It is because
of Your love that I will wait patiently.

O for that to truly be the way I pray.

Walk with Him! Be blessed!

The next day Moses took his place to judge the people. People were standing before him all day long, from morning to night. When Moses' father-in-law saw all that he was doing for the people, he said, "What's going on here? Why are you doing all this, and all by yourself, letting everybody line up before you from morning to night?" Moses said to his father-in-law, "Because the people come to me with questions about God. When something comes up, they come to me. I judge between a man and his neighbor and teach them God's laws and instructions." Moses' father-in-law said, "This is no way to go about it. You'll burn out, and the people right along with you. This is way too much for you—you can't do this alone. Now listen to me. Let me tell you how to do this so that God will be in this with you. Be there for the people before God, but let the matters of concern be presented to God. Your job is to teach them the rules and instructions, to show them how to live, what to do. And then you need to keep a sharp eye out for competent men—men who fear God, men of integrity, men who are incorruptible—and appoint them as leaders over groups organized by the thousand, by the hundred, by fifty, and by ten. They'll be responsible for the everyday work of judging among the people. They'll bring the hard cases to you, but in the routine cases they'll be the judges. They will share your load and that will make it easier for you. If you handle the work this way, you'll have the strength to carry out whatever God commands you, and the people in their settings will flourish also."

—Exodus 18:13–23 (MSG)

The Lord gives you direction. You start following it. Before you realize it, the direction has become much bigger than you—or your pride has gotten in the way. Rather than taking time to adjust to the growth, you just keep trying to keep up with keeping up, never thinking to adjust or drop your pride or control in order to let others help you.

Why is relinquishing control a good thing? It is good for a couple of reasons, as follows: (1) It requires us to trust God to provide someone else who will play the role that we have come to think only we can play. ("God told me to do this, so He must have meant for me to do it, right?") (2) It makes us admit that we are only capable of doing so much and that we need others in our life to complete what we are called to do. God doesn't call us to do very much on our own. When we do more than required, we become burned out and miss out on the joy of honoring Him with our life.

When following God's direction, don't become so wrapped up in following His instructions that you miss the adjustments He sends your way.

Walk with Him! Be blessed!

But let all who take refuge in you rejoice; let them sing joyful praises forever. Spread your protection over them, that all who love your name may be filled with joy.

—Psalms 5:11 (NLT)

I love the promise in this verse: God's protection will be spread over us, and when we love His name, we will be filled with joy. The beginning of the verse is also very important. It reads, "Let all who take refuge in the Lord rejoice." We need to make sure we are taking refuge in the Lord. If we aren't, then we will miss out on the peace, joy, and protection He has surrounded us with.

When times are hard, where do you run to first, to friends, family, social media? Do they point you to Christ, or do you hear solutions that may give you a quick fix but then you find yourself back where you were? Sometimes we miss important parts of Scripture in order to get to the parts we like. Knowing that we are covered in His protection is amazing, but we have to be inside His protection first by taking refuge in what is always present as we walk with Him.

Be blessed!

When the people saw how long it was taking Moses to come back down the mountain, they gathered around Aaron. "Come on," they said, "make us some gods who can lead us. We don't know what happened to this fellow Moses, who brought us here from the land of Egypt." So Aaron said, "Take the gold rings from the ears of your wives and sons and daughters, and bring them to me." All the people took the gold rings from their ears and brought them to Aaron. Then Aaron took the gold, melted it down, and molded it into the shape of a calf. When the people saw it, they exclaimed, "O Israel, these are the gods who brought you out of the land of Egypt!" Aaron saw how excited the people were, so he built an altar in front of the calf. Then he announced, "Tomorrow will be a festival to the Lord!"

—Exodus 32:1–5 (NLT)

Wow! When I read this, I think that we today are very much like the Israelites. God had definitely shown Himself through Moses's delivering the Israelites out of bondage. In the verses before the ones above, God gave very clear instructions to the Israelites about what was expected while He had Moses come up the mountain to give him His Word. And during the forty days when Moses was on the mountain, the Israelites became very impatient. They started to look elsewhere for something to guide them. They even made their own god out of their own stuff (in other words, they tried to make God be what they thought God should be). Hmm, sounds a lot like us, doesn't it? We are so quick to run toward a quick fix that lets us have our way instead of waiting patiently for God's timing. O Lord, You are so patient with us. Thank You!

Walk with Him! Be blessed!

Don't you realize that this sin is like a little yeast that spreads through the whole batch of dough?

—1 Corinthians 5:6 (NLT)

The book of 1 Corinthians definitely draws a line between Christ and the world. I struggle with defending the Word of God and not coming across as judgmental, as the world tends to make me feel. The interesting thing is that Paul isn't talking to nonbelievers in this book of the Bible. He is actually addressing the church at Corinth, a body of believers. It is interesting to me that even in defending the Word to other believers in today's world, I am made to feel judgmental (which is totally my issue, not the Word's). This brings me to the verse above, which is a great example of what happens when we are not careful with the things we have allowed to become a part of our choices and decisions. You see, the feelings I am entertaining are like yeast (pride) in my life. The yeast spreads throughout the dough, causes it to swell, and gives it a completely new look. The same will happen in my life if I don't guard my heart and defend the Word out of love for Christ, not out of pride for what I know about Christ.

By the way, I don't find it to be any type of coincidence that one of the last chapters of 1 Corinthians is the Love Chapter. God's Word is amazing. He not only gives us clear instruction about what He desires for our life (namely, a relationship with Him through His Son, Jesus Christ), but He also tells us how we are to live out that relationship.

Walk with Him! Be blessed!

During that time the devil came and said to him, "If you are the Son of God, tell these stones to become loaves of bread." But Jesus told him, "No! The Scriptures say, 'People do not live by bread alone, but by every word that comes from the mouth of God.'" Then the devil took him to the holy city, Jerusalem, to the highest point of the Temple, and said, "If you are the Son of God, jump off! For the Scriptures say, 'He will order his angels to protect you. And they will hold you up with their hands so you won't even hurt your foot on a stone.'" Jesus responded, "The Scriptures also say, 'You must not test the Lord your God.'"

—Matthew 4:3–7 (NLT)

Most everyone is familiar with Christ's being tempted by Satan after the former spent forty days in the wilderness. Christ quoted Scripture to counter Satan's attacks. What jumped out at me when I read the above verses was the ways in which Satan tried to make Christ question who He is. Twice he said, "If you are the Son of God, then ..." And of course Christ knew who He was and immediately shut down any thought that Satan was trying to use to convince Him otherwise. But how many times do we keep entertaining those thoughts that are brought to us in order to get us to doubt or forget who we are in Christ? Life gets rough, life doesn't go as planned, the unexpected happens, people hurt us, and then we hear the voice say, "If you truly are a child of God, then ..." Wow! Just like Christ, we need to know who we are (in Him). We also need to know Scriptures in order to shut down those thoughts that are not from God.

Walk with Him! Be blessed!

And He said, "My presence shall go with you, and I will give you rest."

—Exodus 33:14 (ESV)

When life gets hectic and we find ourselves in a deep valley, looking up is the thing we do to find our peace and rest in what we know to be true. This helps us seek the presence of the Lord so that He will give us the hope of getting out of the valley. When we are on top of a mountain and life is grand, looking up is the thing to do to thank the Lord for our peace and rest and to praise Him, as we hope to remain there. We just seem closer to our heavenly Father when we are on the mountaintop or even in the valley. On the mountaintop, we call to Him from a heart full of thanksgiving; in the valley, we call to Him from a heart of full of desperation.

The interesting thing, though, is that most of life isn't spent on the mountaintop or in the valley (praise the Lord for that). Most of life is lived on the plains. The terrain may change from desert to grassland to refreshing rivers, but still it is right in the middle, where it is easy to find ourselves not looking up as much as we are looking around. This leads us to wonder, in the midst of all we see, *Where is the Lord?* Whether we are on a mountaintop, in a valley, or on the plains of life, the Lord is with us and gives us rest. We just have to continue to look up and walk with Him.

Be blessed!

We can make our plans, but the Lord determines our steps.

—Proverbs 16:9 (NLT)

So we have our day all planned out—drop the kids off at 8:00; get the car to the oil-change place by 8:30; be back at the house by 10:00; start packing for the baseball tournament this weekend; etc.—but then, bam!, none of that comes to be. Our plans go totally off track. Nothing gets done as scheduled; we get frazzled and frustrated; and the rest of the day is a washout. Maybe we should take the little nuisances of the day and, instead of letting them get the best of us, use them as reminders of who God is, thanking Him for using these small things of life to remind us of the truly big thing He wants us to know: *that He is in control!* Even in the midst of our daily small things, He wants to be praised and remembered. We may think we have our life scheduled out, but the little adjustments can actually be fun reminders that we don't. Interruptions to our schedule remind us that we serve a God who does have everything planned out. Walk with Him! Be blessed!

Be angry and do not sin; do not let the sun go down on your anger, for anger gives a foothold to the devil.

—Ephesians 4:26–27 (ESV)

Blessed are the peacemakers, for they shall be called sons of God.

—Matthew 5:9 (ESV)

What causes quarrels and what causes fights among you? Is it not this, that your passions are at war within you? You desire and do not have, so you murder. You covet and cannot obtain, so you fight and quarrel. You do not have, because you do not ask. You ask and do not receive, because you ask wrongly, to spend it on your passions. You adulterous people! Do you not know that friendship with the world is enmity with God? Therefore whoever wishes to be a friend of the world makes himself an enemy of God. Or do you suppose it is to no purpose that the Scripture says, "He yearns jealously over the spirit that he has made to dwell in us"?

—James 4:1–6 (ESV)

Leave your gift there before the altar and go. First be reconciled to your brother, and then come and offer your gift.

—Matthew 5:24 (ESV)

The first two Scriptures above tell us that being at peace with others is how God desires us to live. The third Scripture, James 4:1–6, tells us why we don't get along with others. The fourth Scripture tells us it is very important to be at peace with others. It says that if we aren't getting along with someone, we should drop everything and take care of the problem. Unfortunately in this world of confrontation we are more than willing to take care of the problem. The problem with this mind-set is that we go to get something settled in order to "win," not to reconcile with the other party. To be able to come to reconciliation, the heart has to have an attitude of "I don't need to win." This doesn't mean you let the other person win; it means that your heart desires reconciliation, or to be brought back into a right relationship with the person, more than being the winner. Look at Christ. It appeared that he had been defeated on the cross, which is very far from the truth. Submitting to crucifixion was just Him giving His will up so that we human beings could be reconciled to God, something we couldn't do on our own. Through what looked like Him not winning was actually Him just surrendering His will to the Father in order to see the greatest victory of all time: the reconciliation of humankind to God. Walk with Him! Be blessed!

Seek the Kingdom of God above all else, and live righteously, and he will give you everything you need.

—Matthew 6:33 (NLT)

The word *seek* appears in the Bible 294 times. That is a lot for one little four-letter word! So there have to be many meanings of this word as it is intended to mean throughout the Word of God. I hear many of us (me included) say, "I am seeking the Lord!" This is great, but then many of us (me included) act like we are playing a game of hide-and-go-seek with the Lord, one wherein Christ is out there hiding and waiting for us to come to find Him so He can give us comfort, peace, wisdom, patience, and—well, it is never ending what we receive from Christ. Then just like in the game, we go hide and close our eyes until it is time to seek Him and find Him again. Well, Christ is never hidden from us, even when we have our eyes covered and we are waiting for the time to go seek Him. Maybe to seek Him means to open our eyes, heart, and mind to His presence and just to see Him in all things.

Walk with Him! Be blessed!

He will lay both of his hands on the goat's head and confess over it all the wickedness, rebellion, and sins of the people of Israel. In this way, he will transfer the people's sins to the head of the goat. Then a man specially chosen for the task will drive the goat into the wilderness. As the goat goes into the wilderness, it will carry all the people's sins upon itself into a desolate land.

—Leviticus 16:21–22 (NLT)

You have probably heard the word *scapegoat*, but do you realize it comes from this passage in the Bible? Yep! This is one of the many instructions given from God to the people of Israel as they were going into the Promised Land. The priest was instructed to take a goat without any blemishes and to place his hands on the goat's head. Then, any despicable thing the people had done (you name it; they had done it) was to be transferred over to the goat, after which time the goat was to be driven away into the wilderness, taking the people's sin far away from them. The goat took the punishment that belonged to the Israelites and removed it. The punishment was separation from the Promised Land, yet the people got to remain there because the scapegoat was removed.

Wow, do you see where this is going? Christ became our "scapegoat" when He suffered and bled on the cross and then went to the grave. He was separated from God so we never have to be. We, because of Christ, get to remain in our Promised Land (our relationship with Christ) and never have to be separated from our heavenly Father while living here on earth or in eternity. Our sin was placed on Christ's head! He was separated from God the Father while in the grave, and then, unlike the goat in the Old Testament, He returned to us, leaving us the Holy Spirit (His presence) once He returned to the Father in eternity. Wow!

Walk with Him! Be blessed!

"They are so deceiving," someone said to me about a group of people, because she knew that the way the group was acting outwardly did not reflect what they held in their hearts. An imaginary line that wasn't being acknowledged was between the groups. Hmm, this is a lot like the *real* line that has been drawn between Christ and the world. Unfortunately we, a lot of the time, act like this line isn't there. most of the time we don't recognize the motives of the side that opposes Christ, which are to kill, steal from, and destroy us so His glory won't be seen. What may appear as enticing, not harmful, and very fun and enjoyable may actually be very deceiving and may be used to draw us into a web of turmoil, heartache, and destruction. In John 10:10 (NIV), Jesus says, "The thief comes only to steal and kill and destroy; I have come that they may have life, and have it to the full." Christ definitely drew the line between Him and the world. Unfortunately, a lot of the time we don't see it or worse know it is there yet don't acknowledge it.

Walk with Him! Be blessed!

Blessed [happy, fortunate, prosperous, and enviable] is the man who walks and lives not in the counsel of the ungodly [following their advice, their plans and purposes], nor stands [submissive and inactive] in the path where sinners walk, nor sits down [to relax and rest] where the scornful [and the mockers] gather. But his delight and desire are in the law of the Lord, and on His law [the precepts, the instructions, the teachings of God] he habitually meditates [ponders and studies] by day and by night [Romans 13:8–10; Galatians 3:1–29; 2 Timothy 3:16]. And he shall be like a tree firmly planted [and tended] by the streams of water, ready to bring forth it's fruit in its season; its leaf also shall not fade or wither; and everything he does shall prosper [and come to maturity] [Jeremiah 17:7–8].

—Psalms 1:1–3 (AB)

There is a lot in these verses. One thing that popped out to me is, "And he shall be like a tree firmly planted by the streams of water ready to bring forth fruit in its season and its leaves shall never wither and everything he does shall prosper." But I simply found no way to use only that verse without providing the others around it. See, first it says to be careful where you are planted, where you walk, and whom you walk with, because "blessed is the man who delights in the ways of the Lord." Then it tells us how to be blessed, and that is by being planted in the Word of God and mediating on the ways of the Lord. This means that we should know and practice His ways. We shouldn't merely agree that they are good things; instead, we should live them—and not just sometimes, but by day and by night. Then the verses tell us how we will be changed by being blessed by the Lord. We will be like a tree that is planted by a water source (God's Word). Because the tree's roots are continually getting nourished by the soil and water (our relationship with Christ), the tree will always be fruitful. Unlike the tree, we don't stay in one place for a lifetime. Even if our geography doesn't change, the people and situations around us do—but our water source and where our roots are established do not change. If we are firmly planted in Christ through belief in who He is, then we will be like a tree planted by a river that can be depended on to produce fruit. We will produce this fruit not so Christ will love us more (He loves us very much, evidenced by the fact that He died for us), but so others will be able to know who Christ is. And because we aren't needed by God to do His work but are invited by Him to be included in His work, this is when we are *blessed*, which brings us back to the beginning of the verses.

Walk with Him! Be blessed!

And I will forgive their wickedness, and I will never again remember their sins.

—Hebrews 8:12 (NLT)

Living in forgiveness is quite interesting. A lot of the time we tend to do it one of two ways: by condemning or by forgetting. Well, at least I have (I can't speak for everyone). See, I have bounced back and forth between two things. One of these things is that I constantly remind Christ of how unforgivable I am. I know and remember my wickedness almost to the point of paralyzing myself. I am afraid to move in fear of messing up and having to ask for forgiveness yet again. The second of these things is that I forget my sin because, well, come on, it wasn't that big of a sin. I mean, I didn't mean to be rude to the cashier at Walmart. I mean, jeez, I was in a hurry and she was the slowest checker ever. And besides, she didn't even smile or look me in the eye. Where is the customer service?

See, I live in condemning or in forgetting, but neither of these is forgiveness. Living in forgiveness comes not from having my wickedness removed but from my understanding of where my forgiveness comes from. I am forgiven because the blood of Jesus was shed on the cross to be the new covenant between us and the Creator, God. The whole chapter of Hebrews 8 explains this one little verse about our sins not being remembered anymore. Verses 1–11 provide the setup for verse 12. In these verses, we are reminded that the old covenant between God and humankind (the one given to Moses) was no longer sufficient because of humankind's wickedness and turning away from God. So God made a final covenant with His creation through Christ, His Son, one that allows our wickedness to be forgiven and remembered no more. He provided this so we can live and walk in the newness of life, not in condemnation or forgetfulness. So if you are struggling with living in forgiveness (which is really about you forgiving yourself), then try living under the forgiveness that was purchased by Christ on the cross. It is because of Him that our sins, no matter their magnitude, can and will be forgiven so we can walk with Him.

Be blessed!

For this reason the Father loves me, because I lay down my life that I may take it up again. No one takes it from me, but I lay it down of my own accord. I have authority to lay it down, and I have authority to take it up again. This charge I have received from my Father."

—John 10:17–18 (ESV)

Think of what the world would be today (if it even still existed) if Christ had chosen something different from what is described in the above verses. I remember when I first realized that Christ had a choice to endure what He endured on the cross, that He didn't just do what He was supposed to do but that He did what He chose to do because of His love for His Father. Wow! Christ knew that the cross was always in His future, and He knew it was still His choice whether or not to be crucified. He chose to be crucified out of love for His Father, which love we now get to receive. This leads me to wonder: *If I knew what my cross of tomorrow would be, would I still carry it?* And just like Christ had a choice, we have a choice. If we have accepted what Christ did on the cross, and if we believe in Him, we don't have to do what we are *supposed* to do because of Him. Instead, we get to *choose* to do what we are asked to do because of our love for Him.

Walk with Him! Be blessed!

God blesses those people who refuse evil advice and won't follow sinners or join in sneering at God. Instead, the Law of the Lord makes them happy, and they think about it day and night. They are like trees growing beside a stream, trees that produce fruit in season and always have leaves. Those people succeed in everything they do. That isn't true of those who are evil, because they are like straw blown by the wind. Sinners won't have an excuse on the day of judgment, and they won't have a place with the people of God. The Lord protects everyone who follows him, but the wicked follow a road that leads to ruin.

—Psalms 1:1–6 (CEV)

There is some harsh stuff in these verses. And there is some very hopeful stuff in these verses too. I find the verses to be really cool, because they show how God definitely draws lines in His Word. These verses paint a clear picture of the difference between a life that is planted in the Word and one that is planted in the world. (And this is very visual thing for me, since the geography of Montana and the geography of the Texas Panhandle are definitely in complete contrast.) A life planted in the world is dry, easily stirred up and blown around, and unsettled, and not much fruit or vegetation can be found in it. A life planted in the Word, which is rooted in the River of Life, is grounded, stable, and fruitful. The winds may still blow, leaves may be lost during certain seasons, and sometimes the tree may look like it is damaged, but because of where its roots are planted, the tree always produces more fruit in the spring, even after a harsh winter. So the question is, where are we planted?

Walk with Him! Be blessed!

Then James and John, the sons of Zebedee, came over and spoke to him. "Teacher," they said, "we want you to do us a favor." "What is your request?" he asked. They replied, "When you sit on your glorious throne, we want to sit in places of honor next to you, one on your right and the other on your left." But Jesus said to them, "You don't know what you are asking! Are you able to drink from the bitter cup of suffering I am about to drink? Are you able to be baptized with the baptism of suffering I must be baptized with?" ... But among you it will be different. Whoever wants to be a leader among you must be your servant, and whoever wants to be first among you must be the slave of everyone else. For even the Son of Man came not to be served but to serve others and to give his life as a ransom for many."

—Mark 10:35–38, 43–45 (NLT)

I won't pretend to know James's and John's motive for asking Jesus to give them a special seat in heaven, but I can say that if this question were asked of Jesus today, the motive would be a little more evident. With social media, television, movies, and sports being so influential in our lives, we are often being presented with the person or happening of the moment. For a lot of us, the struggle is not that we actually admire the person of the moment but that we want what the person seems to have (and what we don't have), which is not so much money and fame as it is the adoration of people. We want people to adore us and to desire to be like us.

Jesus was the talk of His day. Word of Him reached many ears. Many came to see Him. Many wanted to be like Him. Or did they just want what He had, the adoration and the attention of people? Ironically, the attention and adoration of people was not what Jesus wanted at all. He wanted people to know who His Father was. It never was about Him. For Christ, it was always about His Father. That is why He said in Matthew 5:16, "In the same way, let your light shine before others, that they may see your good deeds and glorify your Father in heaven." Walk with Him! Be blessed!

Why sayest thou, O Jacob, and speakest, O Israel, My way is hid from Jehovah, and the justice due to me is passed away from my God? Hast thou not known? hast thou not heard? The everlasting God, Jehovah, the Creator of the ends of the earth, fainteth not, neither is weary; there is no searching of his understanding. He giveth power to the faint; and to him that hath no might he increaseth strength. Even the youths shall faint and be weary, and the young men shall utterly fall: but they that wait for Jehovah shall renew their strength; they shall mount up with wings as eagles; they shall run, and not be weary; they shall walk, and not faint.

—Isaiah 40:27–31 (ASV)

We grow tired and weary in life, especially when we run ahead of the Lord. But when we wait for the Lord to move and we go according to His timing, we will be renewed and not grow weary. Wait on Him and walk with Him. Be blessed!

Teach those who are rich in this world not to be proud and not to trust in their money, which is so unreliable. Their trust should be in God, who richly gives us all we need for our enjoyment. Tell them to use their money to do good. They should be rich in good works and generous to those in need, always being ready to share with others. By doing this they will be storing up their treasure as a good foundation for the future so that they may experience true life. Timothy, guard what God has entrusted to you. Avoid godless, foolish discussions with those who oppose you with their so-called knowledge. Some people have wandered from the faith by following such foolishness. May God's grace be with you all.

—1 Timothy 6:17–21 (NLT)

Money is one of the world's great divides. Yet the problem isn't really money. It is our view of people with or without money. The verses above help us to see that it isn't the presence or absence of money in our lives that makes the difference. It is what we do with what God has entrusted us with that makes the difference. If He has trusted you with a little, then guard your heart so that others are blessed through what you have been entrusted with. If He has trusted you with a lot, then guard your heart so that others are blessed with what you have been entrusted with. Either way, it is about protecting what God has entrusted you with so that others will be blessed. "Tell them to use their money to do good. They should be rich in good works and generous to those in need, always being ready to share with others."

Walk with Him! Be blessed!

> But as for you, continue in what you have learned and have become convinced of, because you know those from whom you learned it, and how from infancy you have known the Holy Scriptures, which are able to make you wise for salvation through faith in Christ Jesus. All Scripture is God-breathed and is useful for teaching, rebuking, correcting and training in righteousness, so that the servant of God may be thoroughly equipped for every good work.

—2 Timothy 3:14–17 (NIV)

Some have had the opportunity to be fed the Word and be taught the things of God from infancy. In the world, this is called "growing up in a Christian home." Some have come to know God later in life. Whenever one comes to know Christ, one still must "grow up" in Christ. In 1 Corinthians 3:2, we are told, "I had to feed you with milk, not with solid food, because you weren't ready for anything stronger. And you still aren't ready." Babies are fed with milk because they are not ready for more complex food. As they grow and their bodies mature, more food can be introduced into their diet. We must grow spiritually, because God can only show us who He is at the level of our understanding (even then, we never become fully mature in Christ while here on earth). We must know the Word of God to grow up in His ways.

Walk with Him! Be blessed!

For as the heavens are higher than the earth, so are my ways higher than your ways and my thoughts than your thoughts.

—Isaiah 55:9 (ESV)

We try hard to think like God thinks, to explain things like God does, and to be in control like God is, but we are not God. No matter how many explanations we can come up with, we will never fully understand the ways of God. Why not? Because equality with God is not attainable by humankind. We are created for God, not to be equal to God. When we begin to understand the love of God, we begin to trust Him. And it is because of our trust in Him that we begin to see His faithfulness to us, which helps us to begin to understand that we are truly created by God for God. Once we believe we are created by Him, we can begin to live for Him.

Walk with Him! Be blessed!

So in everything, do unto others what you would have them do to you, for this sums up the Law and the Prophets.

—Matthew 7:12 (NIV)

Disappointment comes when expectations are not met. Frustration sets in when disappointment comes because expectations are not met. Anger overtakes us when frustrations grow from the disappointment of expectations not being met. Hurt is caused from the anger that comes from the frustration of the disappointment of expectations not being met. Relationships are broken from the hurt done by the anger that arises from the frustration of continued disappointment of expectations not being met. Maybe if our expectations were more focused on what we expected from ourselves, then this cycle could be stopped. I believe it is said best in the golden rule: do unto others as you would have them do unto you.

Walk with Him! Be blessed!

"My thoughts are nothing like your thoughts," says the Lord. "And my ways are far beyond anything you could imagine. For just as the heavens are higher than the earth, so my ways are higher than your ways and my thoughts higher than your thoughts."

—Isaiah 55:8–9 (NLT)

I love how the Lord works. However, if someone asked me how He works, I am not sure I could explain it, because He has been very creative in how He has worked in my life. When I needed more information, He has given it to me. When I needed to be shown what wasn't the direction I had been given, sometimes that came through His letting me go in the wrong direction so I could learn the difference between His will and my wants. Whatever way He has shown Himself to me, it has required the same thing from me: trust. Trust in Him! When my trust in God is in place, my not fully understanding doesn't keep me from fully trusting Him. Trust must come first for understanding to come. If we wait until we understand, then trust will never come. We are asked to trust, not to understand.

Walk with Him! Be blessed!

My dear brothers and sisters, take note of this: Everyone should be quick to listen, slow to speak and slow to become angry, because human anger does not produce the righteousness that God desires. Therefore, get rid of all moral filth and the evil that is so prevalent and humbly accept the word planted in you, which can save you.

—James 1:19–21 (NIV)

Have you ever awakened on edge and known it was going to be one of those days? As this verse says, on these sorts of occasions you are all jumbled up, slow to listen, quick to speak, and even quicker to become angry, totally not wearing the righteousness of God. You take on the filth and evil of the world because you awoke closer to the world than to the Word planted by God in your life. This is where the word *humbly* comes into play. It is in humility that we remember who Christ is and what He did, as compared to who we are and what we do, and that this will get us from where we awoke to where Christ wants to take us on this very day that the Lord has made. Let Christ save your day. Walk with Him! Be blessed!

"Teacher, which is the greatest commandment in the Law?" Jesus replied: "'Love the Lord your God with all your heart and with all your soul and with all your mind.' This is the first and greatest commandment. And the second is like it: 'Love your neighbor as yourself.' All the Law and the Prophets hang on these two commandments."

—Matthew 22:36–40 (NIV)

The people asking Jesus this question were rule followers. They knew the rules of the system forward and backward, so I am not sure why they felt the need to ask the guy who spoke much differently from anyone who had ever spoken before which was the greatest rule (and they had a bunch) to follow. Maybe it was to open up another argument with Jesus; who knows? But it is very cool how Jesus kept His answer plain and simple: "Love the Father with everything you have," following that up with, "Love the person next to you just like you love yourself." Hold on, even people in biblical times struggled with being selfish and putting themselves before others? Such must have been the case, because Jesus says so right here. Jesus says, "You know how to love yourself; now do the same to those around you. Do it second, because your love for God is first and your love of others is next. If you have to include yourself in there, then you should be third."

Walk with Him! Be blessed!

I will sing of your love and justice, lord. I will praise you with songs. I will be careful to live a blameless life—when will you come to help me? I will lead a life of integrity in my own home.

—Psalms 101:1–2 (NLT)

God called David "a man after My own heart." God said this about David because David desired to praise and honor his God with his life. David knew that his life should be one that honored the One he served. And he had an understanding of how that should look. He desired to live a life that at all times honored God, even when he was behind closed doors in his home, where others couldn't see. He was committed to a life of honor, not for himself but for his God. His home was a picture of his heart. David didn't just say and do the right things because he was king and because good behavior was expected from the king. He desired to say and do the right things because of his love for God. So, do we serve God out of obligation (i.e., do we think this is what we are supposed to do because we are Christians), or do we serve God from a heart that desires to honor and praise the One who gave His all? David served from the latter type of heart, which is why God said David "is a man after My own heart." Because God is love and His design comes from His love, when we serve out of love we will be called a person after God's own heart.

Walk with Him! Be blessed!

"Teacher," they said, "we know how honest you are. You are impartial and don't play favorites. You teach the way of God truthfully. Now tell us—is it right to pay taxes to Caesar or not? Should we pay them, or shouldn't we?" Jesus saw through their hypocrisy and said, "Why are you trying to trap me? Show me a Roman coin, and I'll tell you." When they handed it to him, he asked, "Whose picture and title are stamped on it?" "Caesar's," they replied. "Well, then," Jesus said, "give to Caesar what belongs to Caesar, and give to God what belongs to God." His reply completely amazed them.

—Mark 12:14–17 (NLT)

When it is early April and we read the above verses, most of us think, *Ugh, I have got to give the government its tax money* and *Oh, man, is He also implying tithing?* One morning, when I heard someone say that to be in authority one must know how to be under authority, these verses came into my mind. Jesus wasn't just talking about paying taxes when He said to give to Caesar what is Caesar's, or about tithing when He said to give God what is God's. He knew it wasn't about who owned the coin. The Pharisees and Herodians were trying to trap Jesus into saying that the Roman government did not have authority over Him, for which they could and would have taken Him to the Roman court immediately. But because Jesus understood what being under the authority of God means, He understood how to be in authority.

Today the world looks for leaders. We study the great leaders, their characteristics, and the things they did that made them be viewed as great leaders. But very seldom, if ever, do we hear of a leader being described as one who understands how to be under authority. Yet the very One whom we claim to follow was the greatest One ever to model being under authority. As parents, we want so desperately for our children to be leaders and not followers. We tell them, "Be a leader, not a follower." We teach them what a leader does and says, but more importantly we should also teach them to be under the authority of Christ—and then the leadership will follow.

Walk with Him! Be blessed!

Don't envy sinners, but always continue to fear the lord. You will be rewarded for this; your hope will not be disappointed. My child, listen and be wise: Keep your heart on the right course.

—Proverbs 23:17–19 (NLT)

This verse counters how the world encourages us, young and old alike, to live. The message from the world isn't that we should envy someone; it is that we should be envied. We should be the one everyone wants to be, or we should have what everyone wants to have. Some commercials use the technique of encouraging people to make their neighbors envious because the former have what the latter want. You are to be envied! If the Lord tells us to not envy, then should we really desire to be envied?

Even when being the example of Christ to others, we sometimes end up promoting ourselves, trying to be the one who was the example that brought someone to Christ instead of letting Christ, who *is* the One, be the one who did so. We are but a part of His grand design, and the part we play is never more than the *designer's*. Christ never asks anyone to envy Him. He asks us to love, follow, believe, and trust Him. We are to share what He has done with anyone we encounter in an attempt to get others to believe in Him and accept His gift of grace. He is the One who was on the cross and in the tomb, and now He *lives* so we can walk in newness of life. Walk with Him! Be blessed!

Jesus told her, "I am the resurrection and the life. Anyone who believes in me will live, even after dying. Everyone who lives in me and believes in me will never ever die. Do you believe this, Martha?"

—John 11:25–26 (NLT)

Jesus Christ is the same yesterday, today, and forever.

—Hebrews 13:8 (NLT)

The message is still the same as it was some two thousand years ago, when Christ came to earth to suffer on the cross to be the One for all. This may not make sense to this world, but in the Word it says, "'My thoughts are nothing like your thoughts,' says the Lord. 'And my ways are far beyond anything you could imagine'" (Isaiah 55:8 NLT). I do know that "I have sinned and have fallen short of the glory of God." I am in need of a Savior. I need to be saved once for eternity and then daily to walk in the newness of life. He died to give life to all who believe in Him. The cross was just the beginning of the newness. Christ died and suffered to give to anyone who believes in Him the newness. The empty tomb is the newness. We can walk daily with Christ, who is alive.

Walk with Him! Be blessed!

The soldiers led Jesus away, and as they were going, they met a man from Cyrene named Simon who was coming into the city from the country. They seized him, put the cross on him, and made him carry it behind Jesus. A large crowd of people followed him; among them were some women who were weeping and wailing for him. Jesus turned to them and said, "Women of Jerusalem! Don't cry for me, but for yourselves and your children."

—Luke 23:26–28 (GNT)

Jesus was beaten, bruised, and bloodied. He appeared so weak that the centurions got someone else to carry the cross He was to be nailed to in order to die an unbearable death that only He could bear. He looked totally defeated, yet He told the people who were weeping and wailing not to cry for Him but to cry for themselves. I ask, "Wait, You are the one headed to the cross and they need to be crying for themselves? How can You say that? Do You not understand Your own circumstances?" Yes, actually Christ did know His circumstances, but more importantly He understood from where His strength came and knew that whatever lay ahead, He had been prepared to endure it by His Father, whose will He was doing.

Don't let the circumstances of your life determine your perspective of the path you are on. It might be the very thing that reminds you of who you are in Christ, from whom your strength comes, or that points out to you a new strength in Christ you never knew you had, which may be revealed in light of the very circumstances you are now faced with—all for the glory of God. Christ's appearing defeated was just an indication that He was one step closer to victory.

Walk with Him! Be blessed!

Even then, many Jewish authorities believed in Jesus; but because of the Pharisees they did not talk about it openly, so as not to be expelled from the synagogue. They loved human approval rather than the approval of God.

—John 12:42–43 (GNT)

These verses are smack-dab in the middle of the verses about the Passover, when Jesus is having the Last Supper with the disciples. Jesus is washing the disciples' feet, dropping prophecies all over the place about the next few days' events. The verses above appear right in the middle of the Easter passage. They are talking about Jesus entering Jerusalem on a donkey. Amid descriptions of the palm leaves being laid down and waved and of people shouting, "Hosanna to the King," the Bible reads (as I paraphrase), "Oh, and there were these people who believed in Jesus but didn't want to get kicked out of the synagogue, so they just acted like they really didn't believe who He was." Not saying "I believe" is not saying "I don't believe," right? Wow. How many of us know that there are many things around us that oppose Jesus, but we don't let anyone know we don't believe in those things? Nor do we admit, "I do believe that Jesus is the risen Lord. I do believe that Jesus is the Way, the Truth, and the Light of the World! Even if it means you will kick me out of the group, I say that Jesus is in whom I have put my hope and trust." A good question to ask yourself is, "Will I risk losing the approval of people in order to serve my Lord and Savior? Or will I be like those who believed in Him yet didn't let anyone know just so they could remain in the group?"

Walk with Him! Be blessed!

Now there was a disciple at Damascus named Ananias. The Lord said to him in a vision, "Ananias." And he said, "Here I am, Lord." And the Lord said to him, "Rise and go to the street called Straight, and at the house of Judas look for a man of Tarsus named Saul, for behold, he is praying, and he has seen in a vision a man named Ananias come in and lay his hands on him so that he might regain his sight." But Ananias answered, "Lord, I have heard from many about this man, how much evil he has done to your saints at Jerusalem. And here he has authority from the chief priests to bind all who call on your name." But the Lord said to him, "Go, for he is a chosen instrument of mine to carry my name before the Gentiles and kings and the children of Israel. For I will show him how much he must suffer for the sake of my name." So Ananias departed and entered the house. And laying his hands on him he said, "Brother Saul, the Lord Jesus who appeared to you on the road by which you came has sent me so that you may regain your sight and be filled with the Holy Spirit."

—Acts 9:10–17 (ESV)

Many times, this passage is looked at as describing Saul's (Paul's) conversion, given that the scales were removed from Saul's eyes and he then had a new, clearer vision of who Christ is. But Ananias also had his "sight" improved. He was seeing Paul from his own perspective, but Christ showed Ananias His perspective of Paul. How many times has our perspective of someone gotten in the way of our seeing that person how Christ sees him or her? If Christ is going to ask us to remove the scales from someone else's eyes, we must first allow Him to remove the scales from our own eyes.

Walk with Him! Be blessed!

In the same way, faith by itself is dead if it doesn't cause you to do any good things.

—James 2:17 (GNT)

This verse, and the ones around it, has probably spurred many conversations. It has divided followers of Christ in many ways. I won't begin to try to explain this verse and those around it, but I am comfortable in mentioning one way in which it wasn't meant to be seen and heard. It was not meant to be a measuring stick by which to measure another person's life. Too many times we look at another person's life and determine the state of his or her relationship with Christ. "If she really believed, then …" I believe that the Bible has a verse to address this phenomenon. It reads, "Why do you look at the speck of sawdust in your brother's eye and pay no attention to the plank in your own eye" (Matthew 7:3 NIV)? We sometimes choose not to share Christ with someone because the person never appears to believe or seems not to want to hear about Him. Just remember that Saul (whose name was later changed to Paul) appeared not to want to hear or see Christ either, but Christ had different plans for his life. If Paul hadn't been present when the disciples were persecuted, if he hadn't seen people standing up for Christ, then he wouldn't have known who had called his name on the road and who had said to him, "Saul, Saul why are you persecuting me" (Acts 22:6)? Because of the testimony of those he had persecuted, he knew who it was that called his name. The Lord was preparing Paul for His calling on his life even when it didn't look like it. Don't let the circumstances of another person's life let you determine the measure of faith he or she possesses or the measure of faith he or she is being prepared to possess.

Walk with Him! Be blessed!

May the God and Father of our Lord Jesus Christ be blessed! He is the compassionate Father and God of all comfort. He's the one who comforts us in all our trouble so that we can comfort other people who are in every kind of trouble. We offer the same comfort that we ourselves received from God. That is because we receive so much comfort through Christ in the same way that we share so many of Christ's sufferings. So if we have trouble, it is to bring you comfort and salvation. If we are comforted, it is to bring you comfort from the experience of endurance while you go through the same sufferings that we also suffer. Our hope for you is certain, because we know that as you are partners in suffering, so also you are partners in comfort.

—2 Corinthians 1:3–7 (CEB)

When we are struggling with a rebellious child, the loss of a loved one, financial problems, or whatever problem life brings our way, our first response is to ask, "Why the suffering or struggles?" I can't explain why a person may be struggling, but I do believe that God takes the things of this life and uses them for His best in our life. "All things happen for the good of those who love Christ and are fitting into His plan" (Romans 8:28). The verses above lead me to believe that we are comforted by Him during all times, the good, the bad, and the ugly. But it is so much more than just our being comforted by Christ. We are now equipped to comfort someone else who is experiencing what we have experienced. We now have the ability to say, "I understand," and to be believed that we do understand. What a blessing, to be able to comfort others like we have been comforted by Christ Himself. When we do this, Christ is blessed. You might be struggling now in some area, but know that at some point, if you are willing, your struggles will be someone else's blessing when you allow Christ to use those struggles in the way that only He can. Walk with Him! Be blessed!

Do your best to present yourself to God as one approved, a worker who does not need to be ashamed and who correctly handles the word of truth. Avoid godless chatter, because those who indulge in it will become more and more ungodly.

—2 Timothy 2:15–16 (NIV)

This verse can be a bit confusing. If not read carefully, it makes it seem like one has to get things right before one can come to God. In reality, Christ wants us to come to Him just as we are, bringing with us the good, the bad, and the ugly. We can come to Him with everything we are.. He wants us to live as everything we are in Him, not as everything we are in the world. If we are children of God, then we should be different from the world. We are to be in the world but not of the world. In giving our life to Him as our Lord and Savior, we become a new creation. How we live our lives in truth is not about showing people how much better we are since we are a child of the Almighty. It is about living in truth and righteousness, because that is how He has made us through His death on the cross.

Walk with Him! Be blessed!

At harvest time, Cain brought a gift to the Lord. He brought some of the food that he grew from the ground, but Abel brought some animals from his flock. He chose some of his best sheep and brought the best parts from them. The Lord accepted Abel and his gift. But he did not accept Cain and his offering. Cain was sad because of this, and he became very angry. The Lord asked Cain, "Why are you angry? Why does your face look sad? You know that if you do what is right, I will accept you. But if you don't, sin is ready to attack you. That sin will want to control you, but you must control it."

—Genesis 4:3–7 (ERV)

Wait, does God prefer meat over veggies? Why did He accept Abel and his offering but not Cain and his offering? This is how I heard it explained by Tommy Politz, Senior Pastor, Hillside Christian Church, Amarillo, Texas. Three keywords jumped out at me when listening to Politz teach this passage: *some, but,* and *best.* See, the verses say that both Cain and Abel brought some of what they had to God for an offering, *but* Cain just brought some whereas Abel brought some of his best. Cain brought some vegetables, presented them to God, and said, essentially, "Here You go. This is what I had left after doing what I needed to do. Now You can choose from what is left over. Take what You want, and I will take the leftovers of the leftovers." Cain probably thought that God would be pretty pleased with him. He had brought something, right?

On the other hand, Abel brought the best of what he had and then said, "Here, Lord, is the best of what I have. It is Yours to choose from. Take what You want and leave me the leftovers!" It isn't that God needs our best and can't or won't do anything with our leftovers. God actually doesn't need anything from us at all, as He is God. Our offerings (not just money) aren't about what we present to God. What matters is our attitude when we present our offerings to God. Therein lies the difference between Cain's and Abel's offerings. God doesn't prefer meat over vegetables, just like He doesn't love one believer over another, but He knows each believer's heart.

Do you really want God to tell you that you did a great job when both you and He know you could have done better? (This is a very popular desire in today's world, by the way.) Is that really the way we will come to know who we are in Christ, by validating less-than-Christlike offerings? I have been challenged numerous times not to be a Cain but to be more like Abel, bringing my best to Him and saying, "Here, Lord, You choose first!"

Walk with Him! Be blessed!

If you fail to do what you know is right, you are sinning.

—James 4:17 (ERV)

Peter and the other apostles replied, "We must obey God, not men."

—Acts 5:29 (GNT)

There are obvious right and wrong choices we are presented with daily. Like C. S. Lewis wrote in his book *Mere Christianity*, there are just some things that everyone, whether believers or not, agrees are right or wrong. Then there are choices that believers are in agreement about when it comes to whether those choices are right or wrong. So whether we choose right, we still agree on the right or the wrong of the choice. For me, some of the most difficult decisions or choices to make are those that are just choices, with nothing wrong with either or any of them, especially when people whom I love and whose opinion I value come into play. Well, this is how my very wise mom told me to tackle those decisions (I have heard her voice many times in my head saying this): "If you are honest with yourself, then you know the choice that needs to be made. The Holy Spirit is directing you. Are you willing to listen to and follow the Holy Spirit, or are you going to listen to the voices of those whose opinions matter more to you and follow their lead?" She taught me that James 4:17 isn't just talking about choosing between right and wrong, but that it's talking about doing what we know is right when it comes down to pleasing God or pleasing humankind.

Walk with Him! Be blessed!

"I am the Lord, and I do not change. That is why you descendants of Jacob are not already destroyed."

—Malachi 3:6 (NLT)

Ouch! In this verse it doesn't sound like God is too happy, does it? "I *am* the Lord, and I *do not* change. That is why you are not already *destroyed*!" Or do the things I've presented in italics indicate the way we tend to read this verse, because we know or feel that God's anger is what we deserve because we always fall short of His glory and the Deceiver is always reminding us of just how short we fall daily? This brings me to a real problem. Too often we read the Word from our perspective, so we hear what is being said through our own voice and mind instead of through the voice in which it was written, which is the voice of God. We need to guard against letting the tone we detect in the Word get in the way of what He is saying to us. In the verse above, God (whether angry or soft) is reminding the descendants of Jacob that He is still present wherever they are and no matter what they have done. He doesn't change just because they (we) do. God is God no matter who we are. Walk with Him! Be blessed!

I praise the Lord because he is good. I praise the name of the Lord Most High.

—Psalms 7:17 (ERV)

Jesus said to him, "Why do you call me good? Only God is good."

—Luke 18:19 (ERV)

Do you ever have times when a word seems to jump out at you when it is used? That word for me is *good*. People, me included, seem to use that word to describe a lot of things.

"How was your day?"

"Good!"

"How are you doing?"

"Good!"

"How did [something] go?"

"Good!"

This leads me to wonder: are we really good, or is using that word our way of saying, "I am just okay. Things are okay. My day was okay"? Saying that things are good sounds a whole lot better than saying that things are okay. But that isn't really what is on my heart about the word *good*. We also use it to describe people. Someone is a "good" kid, a "good" person, "good"-hearted, and so on. One time a friend of mine who had the task of disciplining high school kids (the official title is assistant high school principal) said to me, "Man, I am so tired of disciplining 'good' kids."

Before I knew it, I had replied, "Then they aren't good kids. Could they be better? Absolutely! But right now they aren't good. We need to stop calling them good when their actions do not merit them being called good." That sounds harsh, I know, but it is true. We sometimes even tell someone who just made a bad decision that he or she is a good person, especially young people. I guess we are afraid of being honest with people and running the risk of hurting their self-esteem. We would rather lie to people and tell them they are good when really they aren't. None of us is good. Even Jesus, when asked a question by a religious leader, asked a question before answering: "Why do you call me good? Only God is good!" The Bible describes us this way: "We are all dirty with sin. Even our good works are not pure. They are like bloodstained rags. We are all like dead leaves. Our sins have carried us away like wind" (Isaiah 64:6 ERV). By continually telling people that they are good when their actions say something else (i.e., they are not being Christlike), we are allowing them to believe a lie, which is that they are good enough not to need a Savior. This is the biggest lie of all, the very lie the world wants them to believe.

Walk with Him! Be blessed!

When Jesus heard this, he told them, "Healthy people don't need a doctor—sick people do. I have come to call not those who think they are righteous, but those who know they are sinners."

—Mark 2:17 (NIV)

Have you ever realized how bad you felt only after you have begun to recover? Let me try that question again. Have you ever been kind of sick, I mean, where you aren't sick enough to stop doing what you are doing so you keep going even though you don't feel good (but not bad enough not to keep going), and then finally you go to a doctor because you just can't shake whatever little thing you have only to realize how bad you really felt once you started getting better? Maybe this is not the case with you, but I have done this a lot of times in my life. I have ignored the fact that there was something physically wrong with me, thinking, *If I just keep going, I will get better. What I am dealing with isn't that big of a deal. Going to the doctor would be silly. I am just not feeling good. I am not really sick.* Only later have I realized that I really was sick and should have gone to the doctor a lot sooner.

Unfortunately I have done this a lot in my walk with Jesus too, going along while knowing something wasn't quite right. But instead of going to Christ, the wonderful healer, I kept pushing through, thinking, *I will get better in time.* What I really needed was to go to Him much sooner. What was wrong wasn't ever something small that would get better in time. It was my pride in thinking that I was righteous already and didn't need Him. All along I was much sicker than I thought I was. I should have gone to Him much, much sooner.

Walk with Him! Be blessed!

On the day the Holy Tent, the Tent of the Agreement, was set up, a cloud covered it. At night the cloud over the Holy Tent looked like fire. The cloud stayed over the Holy Tent all the time. And at night the cloud looked like fire. When the cloud moved from its place over the Holy Tent, the Israelites followed it. When the cloud stopped, that is the place where the Israelites camped. This was the way the Lord showed the Israelites when to move and when to stop and set up camp. While the cloud stayed over the Holy Tent, the people continued to camp in that same place. Sometimes the cloud would stay over the Holy Tent for a long time. The Israelites obeyed the Lord and did not move. Sometimes the cloud was over the Holy Tent for only a few days. So the people obeyed the Lord's command—they followed the cloud when it moved. Sometimes the cloud stayed only during the night—the next morning the cloud moved. So the people gathered their things and followed it. If the cloud moved, during the day or during the night, they followed it. If the cloud stayed over the Holy Tent for two days, a month, or a year, the people stayed at that place. They did not leave until the cloud moved. When the cloud rose from its place and moved, they also moved. So the people obeyed the Lord's commands. They camped when the Lord told them to, and they moved when he told them to. They watched carefully and obeyed the Lord's commands to Moses.

—Numbers 9:15–23 (ERV)

I have heard, read, and studied the story of the Israelites being brought out of bondage from Egypt and taken into the Promised Land many, many times. For the most part, when I thought about this part of the Bible, I focused on how it was only an eleven-day journey, yet because of the Israelites' disobedience it took forty years! I also focused on how whiney the Israelites were. But one time, what jumped out at me was the obedience and patience the Israelites did show when it came to following the Lord's direction. When the cloud moved, they moved; when the cloud stayed, they stayed. Did you notice that sometimes they stayed in one place overnight, for a couple of months, or even for a year? The deal is that they knew the cloud was the Lord's direction, so they followed it and let Him tell them when to move forward, toward His promises. Maybe it isn't that the Lord isn't giving us direction when we are having times when it seems like all we are doing is waiting on the Lord. Maybe we aren't recognizing the "cloud" He has provided so that we would know when to move and when to wait.

Walk with Him! Be blessed!

Do not be anxious about anything, but in everything by prayer and supplication with thanksgiving let your requests be made known to God. And the peace of God, which surpasses all understanding, will guard your hearts and your minds in Christ Jesus. Finally, brothers, whatever is true, whatever is honorable, whatever is just, whatever is pure, whatever is lovely, whatever is commendable, if there is any excellence, if there is anything worthy of praise, think about these things. What you have learned and received and heard and seen in me—practice these things, and the God of peace will be with you.

—Philippians 4:6–9 (ESV)

When feeling anxious or unsteady, I find that Philippians 4:6–7 is my go-to. Reading these verses, repeating them, and meditating on them, I usually end up waiting on the peace to come. I wait and wait, all the while still feeling anxious and unsteady. This is probably because I was just doing the "what" we are to do in those times and not the "how" we are to do it in that time, which is told to us in the next two verses. To overcome anxiousness and unsteadiness, we must think on other things besides what is making us anxious and unsteady. We must think on the truth, not on the lies that could be causing our emotions. We must think of honorable things like our Lord and Savior, who deserves to be honored. We must think on things that are pure. Once again, our Lord and Savior is the only One who was pure and unblemished so as to be the blood sacrifice for us. We must think on things that are lovely, like the beautiful creation of life, both humankind and nature, the latter of which God gave us to enjoy. We must think of things that can be commended because they honor God and all He is. We must think on things of excellence, like the promises of God, who always promises and gives us His best. And most importantly, we must think of things that are praiseworthy, which is Christ and Christ alone, who is the only one or thing worthy of praise, as all things are created through and for Him (Colossians 1:15). While doing all this thinking, we are to put into practice what we have been taught, what we have received, read, and seen through Scripture, prayer, and other believers, and then the assurance of the God of peace will be with us.

Walk with Him! Be blessed!

Love is patient and kind. Love is not jealous, it does not brag, and it is not proud. Love is not rude, it is not selfish, and it cannot be made angry easily. Love does not remember wrongs done against it. Love is never happy when others do wrong, but it is always happy with the truth. Love never gives up on people. It never stops trusting, never loses hope, and never quits. Love will never end. But all those gifts will come to an end—even the gift of prophecy, the gift of speaking in different kinds of languages, and the gift of knowledge. These will all end because this knowledge and these prophecies we have are not complete. But when perfection comes, the things that are not complete will end.

—1 Corinthians 13:4–10 (ERV)

Each year when it is Valentine's Day, the Love Chapter of the Bible must be read. I love this chapter. It reminds me not only how I am loved but also, and most important, how I am to love. All throughout Scripture, we see and are shown that Christ is love. He is the fulfillment of God's love. "For God so loved the world He gave His only begotten Son that who so ever believeth in Him shall not perish and will have everlasting life." (John 3:16 KJV). One thing that Scripture may not say about love but that is shown throughout Scripture is the fact that love is unique. Christ not only showed love to people but also uniquely loved them. Christ loved those around Him exactly how they needed to be loved. To the woman at the well, He showed she was loved no matter her background. To Zacchaeus, He gave love by spending time with him at his house. For Lazarus it was the love of healing and being brought back to life. I could go on and on about the unique ways Christ showed His love to people. To love uniquely like Christ must take a lot of energy, but it is the kind of love He demonstrated to us and the kind of love we should demonstrate to others. How can we love each person individually? Well, by knowing that we are all so much alike. We are all in need of the Savior. We love uniquely so our one common need can be met.

Walk with Him! Be blessed!

His lord said unto him, Well done, good and faithful servant: thou hast been faithful over a few things, I will set thee over many things; enter thou into the joy of thy lord.

—Matthew 25:23 (ASV)

This verse is one of my favorites. It is part of the parable of the talents. Three men were each given a different number of talents, five, two, and one. The man with five and the man with two both doubled the number of talents, so they had twice as many to give back to their master. The man who had one talent buried it and only had the original one to return to his master. The two who had doubled the talents were told, "Well done, good and faithful servant: thou hast been faithful over a few things, I will set thee over many things; enter thou into the joy of thy lord" (Matthew 25:23). As for the other one, well, let's just say that his master's response wasn't pretty.

This is how I have come to see the talents. They are like the little things of life. As a matter of fact, they may not seem to matter much. I mean, what if I am a little late to work? Or what if I twist the truth about why my assignment that was due is late? I still got it turned in. It was completed, just not in time. Also, does it really matter if I repeat gossip and maybe even embellish it a bit so I can be the one who really seems to be in the know? And I know I have a temper, but come on, if people didn't irritate me so much, I wouldn't lose it. These are just a few of the ways I justify not being disciplined in the "little" things of life.

Well, if we can't be trusted with the little choices and decisions we make each day, things that would honor the kingdom of God if we chose correctly, then how can we be trusted with the big responsibilities of the kingdom? I had someone tell me once that she had tried to teach her children never to let the little things become big things—or, as said above, "If you can be trusted with a few things, then you can be trusted with many." Many of us want God to use us in mighty ways and we just don't understand why He hasn't yet. Maybe we need to be faithful in the things we tend to overlook as not being a big deal. Maybe God is waiting for us to go dig up the one talent we have been trusted with and turn it into two.

Walk with Him! Be blessed!

Jesus saith unto him, I am the way, and the truth, and the life: no one cometh unto the Father, but by me.

—John 14:6 (ASV)

Jesus is the only one who can save people. His name is the only power in the world that has been given to save anyone. We must be saved through him!"

—Acts 4:12 (ERV)

My family spent one Christmas in a different state. While we were walking around Walmart, something jumped out at me and my daughters. While there were lights, trees, and Santa Claus, there was no Jesus. So me being me, I asked, "Where is baby Jesus?" Yes, I was being silly, but I was also being very serious. I saw an absence of Jesus in Christmas. Then it hit me: that is how so many people are trying to have a relationship with God. The world allows and even encourages people to find a god even if they have to make one up, but if you include Jesus in that relationship, you are going too far in your beliefs. You can be very "spiritual," but you mustn't be a Christian. And it is cool to be searching for something, but you should stop short of finding Jesus, because that, well, just makes people a little too uncomfortable. When Jesus comes into the picture, the world has to admit it doesn't have the answers. It can't explain everything, and that is something world doesn't like admitting. When we consider Jesus, we face our sinful selves and our need for a Savior, whereas the world wants us to believe that we can do things on our own and don't need to be saved. When we consider Jesus, we realize we can't do it on our own and that we need to humbly come to Him, but the world says, "You don't need anyone; you have yourself." When you consider Jesus, you find the relationship for which you were created, whereas the world says, "Relationships are only good for a while, so keep searching. There is something better out there."

So I pose a couple of questions: If you have entered into a relationship with Christ, how do you consider Him daily, in ways that make the world comfortable or uncomfortable? If you haven't entered into a relationship with Jesus, will you consider Him to see who He is? Because He really is the difference maker. Even the world agrees on that.

Walk with Him! Be blessed!

Be still, and know that I am God: I will be exalted among the heathen, I will be exalted in the earth.

—Psalms 46:10 (KJV)

If someone were to ask me where I am in my relationship with the Lord, this is the verse I would quote, and I would probably say it this way: "Be still and know that I am God," meaning that nothing big and nothing small is really going on; I am just doing what I do daily, living, working, and hopefully bringing glory to Him who is the only One who deserves praise. Sure, I have some desires I would like to see come to be, but there is nothing urgently needed or something that needs to be fixed. I am enjoying the peace and the calm of this time, but I also know I must guard against becoming lazy during this time. For it is in these downtimes that it is easy for me to stop seeking His will and to just coast. It is in these downtimes that it becomes easy to begin giving Him less and to begin giving more to the distractions around me. That is where "being still and knowing that He is God" needs to be paired with Proverbs 4:23: "Guard your heart above all else, for it determines the course of your life." There is a second part to the verse "Be still and know I am God," and that is, "I will be exalted among the heathen and among the earth." So when nothing "big" is going on in our lives and we are at a place where we can "be still and know that He is God," we are still to be exalting Him above all else. We must guard our hearts from thinking that this is our vacation from bringing glory to God since nothing crazy is going on and, thereby, making those times about us. It is never about us but always about Him and His glory. Walk with Him! Be blessed!

People insulted him, but he did not insult them back. He suffered, but he did not threaten anyone. No, he let God take care of him. God is the one who judges rightly. Christ carried our sins in his body on the cross. He did this so that we would stop living for sin and live for what is right. By his wounds you were healed. You were like sheep that went the wrong way. But now you have come back to the Shepherd and Protector of your lives.

—1 Peter 2:23–25 (ERV)

People hurt people. Our sinful nature causes damage not only to our relationship with Christ but also to our relationships with people. Many times, hurts and damages from early in our lives are still causing us struggles many years later, even if we are no longer around, or associate with, the ones who hurt us so deeply. Unfortunately, we continue to be affected by their actions. Many times we don't even realize that their actions are the source of our difficulties and that our actions only complicate our struggles. We see our struggles as something that we caused and therefore as something we can fix. If we are just good enough, then life won't be so hard. If we just pray and read our Bible enough, then life will be easy and as we desire it to be. If we are aware of the source of our struggles, then we might even think we can prove how wrong those people were ever to hurt us by being more successful than they are, more important than they are, and even more righteous than they are. In other words, we will make sure our enemies know they messed with the wrong person.

But the verses above tell us that if we are behaving this way, we are looking for healing in all the wrong places. Christ didn't insult back when insults were thrown His way. Christ didn't strike back when He was struck. Christ didn't live His life to prove Himself to anyone or to overcome (and thereby better Himself by) the pain the world caused, because He knew God would take care of Him. Christ's knowing that God would never fail Him didn't remove the cross from Christ's life, but it was what gave Him the strength to endure the cross.

What are you still trying to fix in your life that the Lord is asking you to give to Him so He can take care of you? He is the protector of our life. This doesn't mean we won't have our own crosses to carry, but it does mean He gives us the strength to carry them just like Christ was given the strength He needed to go to the cross. He was able to do so because He knew that God would take care of Him.

Walk with Him! Be blessed!

> Don't change yourselves to be like the people of this world, but let God change you inside with a new way of thinking. Then you will be able to understand and accept what God wants for you. You will be able to know what is good and pleasing to him and what is perfect.

—Romans 12:2 (ERV)

The estimated number of self-help books that have been written within the last, oh, ten years is 1,563,789 and counting. (This number has not been verified. As a matter of fact, I just made it up. This is ironic considering that I am writing this book. But note that this is not a self-help book. Its purpose is to point whoever reads it to the Word of God, which is the living, breathing testament of Him.) It seems that every time I turn around, someone has discovered a new way to help others improve some area of their life that is currently lacking. The crazy thing is that you might not have even known that whatever it is was lacking if someone hadn't written a book to tell you that this area of your life was lacking, which sent you into an immediate "I've got to get this fixed" mode. You may have thought that if you didn't get the matter fixed, then your life would never be what it was intended to be. Then someone else writes another book, and you discover another area your life that needs improving. The cycle goes on and on.

Well, my friend, someone has written a book—and it is not the newest on the market—describing an area of our lives that needs fixing. As a matter of fact, this book has been around for thousands of years. The message about the area of our life that needs improvement has remained the same since the day it was *spoken* into writing by God. The message is this: we are in need of a Savior, and it isn't ourselves.

> For God so loved the world [the world created by Him] that He gave His only begotten Son [who was with Him when He created the world] that who so ever [any man, woman, or child] believes in Him [Jesus who was born of a virgin, lived and breathed on this earth, the perfect Son of God, died on the cross and rose from the grave defeating death, appeared

to hundreds over forty days then taken up to heaven, where He now sits at the right hand of His holy Father] shall not perish but have eternal life! (John 3:16 AMP)

You can keep reading all the self-help books you want, and your life will probably improve some. But if the Holy Word of God is not on your list, then you might want to give it some reading and study time. I recommend it because, unlike the books of this world, which keep changing the messages, God's Word has been constant since the day He wrote it. As Romans 12:2 reads, "Don't change yourselves to be like the people of this world, but let God change you inside with a new way of thinking. Then you will be able to understand and accept what God wants for you. You will be able to know what is good and pleasing to Him and what is perfect."

Walk with Him! Be blessed!

Who really believed what we heard? Who saw in it the Lord's great power? He was always close to the Lord. He grew up like a young plant, like a root growing in dry ground. There was nothing special or impressive about the way he looked, nothing we could see that would cause us to like him. People made fun of him, and even his friends left him. He was a man who suffered a lot of pain and sickness. We treated him like someone of no importance, like someone people will not even look at but turn away from in disgust. The fact is, it was our suffering he took on himself; he bore our pain. But we thought that God was punishing him, that God was beating him for something he did. But he was being punished for what we did. He was crushed because of our guilt. He took the punishment we deserved, and this brought us peace. We were healed because of his pain. We had all wandered away like sheep. We had gone our own way. And yet the Lord put all our guilt on him. He was treated badly, but he never protested. He said nothing, like a lamb being led away to be killed. He was like a sheep that makes no sound as its wool is being cut off. He never opened his mouth to defend himself. He was taken away by force and judged unfairly. The people of his time did not even notice that he was killed. But he was put to death for the sins of his people. He had done no wrong to anyone. He had never even told a lie. But he was buried among the wicked. His tomb was with the rich. But the Lord was pleased with this humble servant who suffered such pain. Even after giving himself as an offering for sin, he will see his descendants and enjoy a long life. He will succeed in doing what the Lord wanted. After his suffering he will see the light, and he will be satisfied with what he experienced. The Lord says, "My servant, who always does what is right, will make his people right with me; he will take away their sins. For this reason, I will treat him as one of my great people. I will give him the rewards of one who wins in battle, and he will share them with his powerful ones. I will do this because he gave his life for the people. He was considered a criminal, but the truth is, he carried away the sins of many. Now he will stand before me and speak for those who have sinned."

—Isaiah 53:1–12 (ERV)

Don't look before answering the question of whether or not you saw where these verses are found in the Bible. Aw, you looked, didn't you? Are you surprised to see that these verses are found in the Old Testament book of Isaiah? They read like they should be in the New Testament, smackdab in the middle of talking about Jesus's life. But here they are in the book of Isaiah in the Old Testament. It is even more amazing when you consider the gap between the writing of the Old Testament and the New Testament. Here are these Words from God about the One who bridges the two. And who is that? Christ! He is the One who provides the bridge so we can cross through Him (and only through Him) and get back into a relationship with our heavenly Father and the Creator of life. Christ was born to die for humankind because of humanity's broken relationship with God, which began in the garden of Eden. This reconciliation was only accomplished because of Christ's willingness to do His Father's will. His Father's will was for Christ to be the blood sacrifice required. He shed His blood, suffered, died, and rose so we can walk back across His bridge and into a perfect relationship with God Almighty. People put Christ on the cross. Our sins nailed Him to it. But His love for the Father and for us kept Him there. In the garden of Gethsemane He prayed, "Not My will but Yours." Then on the cross He cried out, "It is finished!" He had done what He had come to do.

Walk with Him! Be blessed!

For their duty was to assist the sons of Aaron for the service of the house of the Lord, having the care of the courts and the chambers, the cleansing of all that is holy, and any work for the service of the house of God. Their duty was also to assist with the showbread, the flour for the grain offering, the wafers of unleavened bread, the baked offering, the offering mixed with oil, and all measures of quantity or size.

—1 Chronicles 23:28–29 (ESV)

The first book of Chronicles is an interesting read as it gives a lot of lists of people and things. Sometimes I wonder why this is so. Why do we need to know these lists of names, most of which I can't pronounce (yes, I am phonetically challenged). But I read a devotional about Chronicles 23 that explained it this way. God listed these people and their duties to help us see that it isn't just the "important" people who further His kingdom. We all further the kingdom with our daily lives. In the verses that appear before the verses above is a list of people who aren't mentioned many other places in the Word, yet they are mentioned here. Why? Maybe to let us know He uses all of us for His glory, not just the Moseses, the Davids the Peters, the Pauls, and the others we see as being the heavy hitters for Christ. Whatever we do, we can bring glory to God the Father by doing what we do to honor Him. We bring Him honor by living like Christ, who lived His life to honor the One who had sent Him. Walk with Him! Be blessed!

And pray for me, too. Ask God to give me the right words so I can boldly explain God's mysterious plan that the Good News is for Jews and Gentiles alike.

—Ephesians 6:19 (NLT)

Paul asked for prayer so that he could boldly explain God's mysterious plan of salvation to the Jews and the Gentiles. How many times in your youth were you told to think before you speak? I was told that a lot. I probably should have been told it even more times. In the verse above, Paul is telling us to do something even more important and wise before speaking. He is telling us to pray before we speak. He advises us to be careful not to allow our zeal for telling others of the good news of Christ and His perfect love to cloud our message. He is saying that we should take the time to pray before we speak. Prayer is the difference maker when it comes to not only how we say something but also how it is received by those who hear what we say. Prayer engages the heart, not just the tongue and the ears. If we prayed more, then we would probably speak less—and what we said would be heard and understood more.

Walk with Him! Be blessed!

You were running the race so well. Who has held you back from following the truth? It certainly isn't God, for he is the one who called you to freedom. This false teaching is like a little yeast that spreads through the whole batch of dough!

—Galatians 5:7–9 (NLT)

Someone pointed this verse out to me. As she was discussing how it spoke to her, I was being convicted as to how it was speaking to me. See, my acquaintance and I were being spoken to in totally different ways. What is even more interesting is that what jumped out at both of us was the same, yet it came across very differently. "Who has held you back from following the truth?" was where both our hearts landed. She was concerned and convicted about being the one who was holding someone else back or running interference between someone and his or her trust and faith in God, and I was being reminded, yet again, "You are getting distracted again, Tammie. This is the same thing we have settled time and time again. Why do you keep going back to that place that runs interference between Me and you, to that thing that costs you so much time and energy and takes all your focus off Me? Do we really have to walk this path again? Are you going to allow it to be as slow and painful as it has been in the past because you are listening to it more than you are listening to Me? Have you forgotten how I set you free from this only for you to pick it up again? Yes, it started small, but now, like yeast spread throughout the entire batch of dough, it is consuming you, so much so that you are forgetting the truths I have shared with and taught to you. You are allowing doubt to creep back in, overshadowing the freedom from this problem that you have received. Okay, if you really want to do this again, we will, because 'I will never leave you or forsake you.' But we don't have to, because you are already free from this."

Whichever way this verse hits home for you, just know it isn't the Lord who is holding you back from running free or causing you to be a distraction for someone else. What is holding you back is that which you have set your sights on, the stuff around you instead of on Him, which, unfortunately, is probably a familiar path—and one you don't have to be on.

Walk with Him! Be blessed!

Not that I have already obtained all this, or have already arrived at my goal, but I press on to take hold of that for which Christ Jesus took hold of me. Brothers and sisters, I do not consider myself yet to have taken hold of it. But one thing I do: Forgetting what is behind and straining toward what is ahead.

—Philippians 3:12–13 (NIV)

Many are living for that time in life when everything comes together—and then they will be able to do something with their lives. But right now things aren't just right. We think that we have to get to a certain point or place and then everything will be in perfect alignment. That is when we think we'll be able to say, "Okay, Lord, ready, set, let's go. I have worked it all out, and now I am ready to do something great for You." Unfortunately there will never be a time when we have everything together and will be perfectly equipped to take hold of what the Lord has for us. And if we continually wait for that perfect time, we run the risk of missing out on His perfect timing in our life. So maybe we should stop waiting for it all to come together. We should know now that He has it all together for us. We just need to surrender to Him and take hold of what He took hold of us for instead of holding onto what we think we have to offer to Him.

Walk with Him! Be blessed!

Yes, they knew God, but they wouldn't worship him as God or even give him thanks. And they began to think up foolish ideas of what God was like. As a result, their minds became dark and confused. Claiming to be wise, they instead became utter fools. And instead of worshiping the glorious, ever-living God, they worshiped idols made to look like mere people and birds and animals and reptiles. So God abandoned them to do whatever shameful things their hearts desired. As a result, they did vile and degrading things with each other's bodies. They traded the truth about God for a lie. So they worshiped and served the things God created instead of the Creator himself, who is worthy of eternal praise! Amen.

—Romans 1:21–25 (NLT)

We need to be careful when we read these verses so we don't automatically think, *Yep, that is what is going on in the world today!* What jumped out at me were the first words of these verses, "Yes, they knew God, but…," which indicates that these verses are not talking about the world but are addressing those who know God: His church, the body of believers, those who proclaim to know Him. We must guard against becoming so caught up in thinking that we are so much better (i.e., being prideful) as individuals and as a group that we begin to worship that which has been created (self) instead of the Creator (God/Christ). If you read on in Romans, then you see that life isn't pretty for those who worship self (the created) over worshiping God Almighty (the Creator). Yes, Scripture talks about the world and things to come, but it talks *to* the church (believers) who are to minister to the hurting world so that they will know of God's love, which caused Him to send His only Son to die on the cross so that *all* who accept the free gift of life through Christ can walk into eternal glory. Walk with Him! Be blessed!

Why can't you understand that I'm not talking about bread? So again I say, "Beware of the yeast of the Pharisees and Sadducees." Then at last they understood that he wasn't speaking about the yeast in bread, but about the deceptive teaching of the Pharisees and Sadducees.

—Matthew 16:11–12 (NLT)

Jesus told many parables when speaking to the people. He would later explain them to the disciples. It is really cool to me how each one of Christ's parables can be applied to believers today. And it is also interesting to me how many times we respond to the parables in the same way the disciples did. Take for example the parable of the yeast being in bread and how we are to be aware of its effects on our life. The disciples automatically began thinking about an immediate need (food) and what they hadn't done to "help" Jesus in meeting that need. Actually, Jesus was addressing something much bigger. It was only after the disciples listened to and questioned Jesus more that they got the real meaning He intended for the parable, which carried an even more important message (beware of the ideas of the world changing up the message of Christ). We must be careful not to merely search God's Word for information about the immediate needs of this world. Instead, we must seek and ask for the eternal message found in His Word.

Walk with Him! Be blessed!

Remember how you made the Lord your God angry in the desert. Never forget that! From the day you left the land of Egypt to the day you came to this place, you have refused to obey the Lord.

—Deuteronomy 9:7 (ERV)

In Deuteronomy 9:1–6, the Israelites are told to go and take the land from the Anakites. "The people there are tall and strong. They are the Anakites. You know about them. You heard our spies say, 'No one can win against the Anakites'" (Deuteronomy 9:2 ERV). That sounds like a battle I wouldn't want to go fight. But the Israelites are told that the Lord will go before them: "But you can be sure that it is the Lord your God who goes across the river before you—and God is like a fire that destroys. He will destroy those nations and make them fall before you. You will force those nations out and quickly destroy them. The Lord has promised you that this will happen" (Deuteronomy 9:3 ERV). Oh, okay, so maybe I would go and fight this battle. But then the Israelites are told not to get too full of themselves because they aren't anything to brag about.

The Lord your God will force those nations out for you. But don't say to yourselves, "The Lord brought us to live in this land because we are such good people." No, the Lord forced those nations out because they were evil, not because you were good. You are going in to take their land, but not because you are good and live right. You are going in, and the Lord your God is forcing those people out because of the evil way they lived. And the Lord wants to keep the promise he made to your ancestors, Abraham, Isaac, and Jacob. (Deuteronomy 9:4–5 ERV)

Ouch! Notice that the Lord is revealing the reason the Israelites get to enter the land in the last part of verse 5: "And the Lord wants to keep the promise He made to your ancestors, Abraham, Isaac, and Jacob." Then the Lord tells them again, "The Lord your God is giving you that good land to live in, but you should know that it is not because you are good. The truth is that you are very stubborn people" (Deuteronomy 9:6)! Ouch again!

This brings us to verse 7, where the Israelites are told, "Remember how you made the Lord your God angry in the desert. Never forget that. From the day you left the land of Egypt to the day you came to this place, you have refused to obey the Lord" (Deuteronomy 9:7 ERV). So if the Israelites were so bad and frustrating to God, then why did they get to enter into the Promised Land? (If you keep reading the chapter, you will discover all the things they did while in the desert.) I guess that the Lord really wanted to make sure that they remembered how many times they had turned their back on Him. Why? So they would enter into the Promised Land with heads hung low and in shame, knowing they didn't deserve the land? I don't believe that is the reason at all. I believe the Lord was telling them to stop focusing so much on themselves and to begin focusing on His faithfulness, goodness, and provision. Because in spite of the Israelites and their actions, the Lord remained faithful to Abraham, Isaac, and Jacob. And because the Israelites could see that He was faithful to a promise made many years ago, they can go boldly into the land with the promise of Him being with them now (see verse 3, where a swift victory is promised). God doesn't want us to remember how we have failed Him so that we walk in shame. He wants us to remember His faithfulness to His promises made to us in spite of our unfaithfulness and our broken promises to Him. Remembering our broken promises reminds us of His unbroken ones, giving us hope and boldness to go into whatever land He is directing us to enter. It isn't about us and what we do or don't do; it is about Him and what He has done and promises to do.

Walk with Him! Be blessed!

After these things God tested Abraham and said to him, "Abraham!" And he said, "Here I am." He said, "Take your son, your only son Isaac, whom you love, and go to the land of Moriah, and offer him there as a burnt offering on one of the mountains of which I shall tell you." So Abraham rose early in the morning, saddled his donkey, and took two of his young men with him, and his son Isaac. And he cut the wood for the burnt offering and arose and went to the place of which God had told him. On the third day Abraham lifted up his eyes and saw the place from afar. Then Abraham said to his young men, "Stay here with the donkey; I and the boy will go over there and worship and come again to you." And Abraham took the wood of the burnt offering and laid it on Isaac his son. And he took in his hand the fire and the knife. So they went both of them together. And Isaac said to his father Abraham, "My father!" And he said, "Here I am, my son." He said, "Behold, the fire and the wood, but where is the lamb for a burnt offering?" Abraham said, "God will provide for himself the lamb for a burnt offering, my son." So they went both of them together. When they came to the place of which God had told him, Abraham built the altar there and laid the wood in order and bound Isaac his son and laid him on the altar, on top of the wood. Then Abraham reached out his hand and took the knife to slaughter his son. But the angel of the Lord called to him from heaven and said, "Abraham, Abraham!" And he said, "Here I am." He said, "Do not lay your hand on the boy or do anything to him, for now I know that you fear God, seeing you have not withheld your son, your only son, from me." And Abraham lifted up his eyes and looked, and behold, behind him was a ram, caught in a thicket by his horns. And Abraham went and took the ram and offered it up as a burnt offering instead of his son. So Abraham called the name of that place, "The Lord will provide"; as it is said to this day, "On the mount of the Lord it shall be provided."

—Genesis 22:1–14 (ESV)

This is my favorite story in the Word about trusting God. Abraham trusted God and His promises so much that even when he was instructed to do something that made no sense to him—to use his promised son for a sacrifice—he did as he had been commanded. Abraham trusted God more than he wanted God's commands to make sense. My sister described this as open-handed trust. Wow, wouldn't it be amazing if we could have open-handed trust like Abraham did? Wouldn't it be great to trust God and to let go of all the things we hold onto in those times when trust is asked of us, not only in the easy daily areas but also in the most difficult areas? Wouldn't it be something to truly give God our open-handed trust because we know what we are told in Isaiah 41:10: "So do not fear, for I am with you; do not be dismayed, for I am your God. I will strengthen you and help you; I will uphold you with my righteous right hand." We are told it again in Isaiah 41:13: "For I am the Lord your God who takes hold of your right hand and says to you, Do not fear; I will help you." So open your hand and give God your open-handed trust, because He has hold of you while you walk with Him.

Be blessed!

Stop deceiving yourselves. If you think you are wise by this world's standards, you need to become a fool to be truly wise. For the wisdom of this world is foolishness to God. As the Scriptures say, "He traps the wise in the snare of their own cleverness."

—1 Corinthians 3:18–19 (NLT)

We need not to confuse maturity with information. We live in a world of information. At an early age, one can gain a plethora of information about various subjects and can sound knowledgeable on a variety of topics. Unfortunately we have come to see young people who do this as being wise or mature for their age. Yet maturity is not solely based on the knowledge one possesses. For me, maturity is better measured by how a person handles the age-appropriate responsibilities he or she is given, by how a person translates the information he or she knows and applies it to the appropriate situation.

Walk with Him! Be blessed!

Jesse sent someone to get his youngest son. This son was a good-looking, healthy young man. He was very handsome. The Lord said to Samuel, "Get up and anoint him. He is the one." Samuel took the horn with the oil in it, and poured the special oil on Jesse's youngest son in front of his brothers. The Spirit of the Lord came on David with great power from that day on. Then Samuel went back home to Ramah.

—1 Samuel 16:12–13 (ERV)

In 1 Samuel 15, Saul had gone against the Lord's commands and had done with the Amalekites as he had seen fit, not as the Lord had instructed. (This is much like what we do today. How many times do we think we need to tweak God's instruction?) God told Samuel that He was removing Saul as king. When applying today's mind-set to these verses, we think that God must mean that such a thing will happen immediately, right? Nope. In God's perfect timing, Saul would be removed from the throne. The Lord sent Samuel to the house of Jesse and told him to anoint those He had told him to anoint. Jesse brought his sons before Samuel. And here are Samuel's thoughts: "When they arrived, Samuel took one look at Eliab and thought, 'Surely this is the Lord's anointed!' But the Lord said to Samuel, 'Don't judge by his appearance or height, for I have rejected him. The Lord doesn't see things the way you see them. People judge by outward appearance, but the Lord looks at the heart'" (1 Samuel 16:6–7 NLT). So on down the line of sons of Jesse Samuel went. He had to ask, "Is that it? Any more sons? Because none of these are who I am to anoint." So Jesse called for his youngest son, David, to come in from the field. Samuel might have thought, *Well, God surely doesn't mean the young son David. He is too young, right?* Nope. God said, "Yes, it is David! He is the one who is to become king." Immediately, right? Nope. All in God's perfect timing. Keep reading first and second Samuel to see how God orchestrated David's becoming king and also becoming a man after His own heart. And while you are reading, remember that God says in many different ways throughout His Word, "My ways are not your ways. My thoughts are not your thoughts. My timing is not your timing."

Walk with Him! Be blessed!

This righteousness is given through faith in Jesus Christ to all who believe. There is no difference between Jew and Gentile, for all have sinned and fall short of the glory of God, and all are justified freely by his grace through the redemption that came by Christ Jesus.

—Romans 3:22–24 (NIV)

One April, I had surgery to repair my rotator cuff. That same year only three months later I slipped and broke my ankle. I know year of injuries. While I was waiting for August 13 to come so I could have surgery on my ankle I had these thoughts. While both injuries required surgery to fix the problems, the way in which each injury came about was quite different. See, the rotator cuff injury was a nagging injury that had been going on for quite a while (ten years at least, maybe longer), but it was never really that bad. I would have times when I knew something wasn't right, but then I would adjust what I was doing and the pain would get better—and then I could resume normal activity. This method worked until one January when I raised my arm and felt something I had never felt before. I knew I couldn't ignore the problem any longer. Now the pain did get better, but because I had experienced something much different, I knew I still needed to see a doctor. So, off to the doctor I went. Surgery was recommended as the only way my shoulder would get better. I put off the surgery for as long as I could and even considered canceling it, because by the time the surgery date rolled around, I had gone back to what I had come to know as my normal. But I had the surgery anyway. And, my goodness, had I known I would feel so much relief throughout my whole body, I would have had the surgery years earlier. But, see, I had become so conditioned to functioning with the pain that it had become what I knew. It had become easy for me to ignore the fact that I needed something fixed. I learned to function, to compensate, and to totally ignore the signals my body was sending to me, indicating that I needed to do something about what was going on.

With my ankle problem, I knew in the instant after taking a single step that I had an injury that couldn't wait to be fixed. As a matter of fact, I was impatient to get the surgery done because I knew that my ankle wouldn't get better without it.

With all that said, it is amazing to me how both situations reflect how many of us respond to the call of the Holy Spirit and come to the realization we have a need to be saved by the saving grace of Christ. Many of us while living life compare ourselves to others and see that it is easy to think we are good even though we know something isn't quite right. We adjust what we do and then things seem to get better, but really nothing has changed. This goes on for years until something different happens and we know and have to admit that we need Jesus. Even after we accept Him and things become normal again, we start thinking that we can do things on your own. But still we say, "Okay, Lord, do the work in me that needs to be done!" Then and only then do we begin to know the difference between us guiding our life and Him guiding our life—and then we say, "Man, I should have allowed Him to be Lord of my life long ago!"

Then there are those of us who have gone along in life thinking that all is good until that one life-changing event happens and we know we are in a place where we can't deny we have a problem. It is then that we cry out to God, because we have no one else to call. We reach the point that we know He is our only refuge. We know we might have to wait to be fixed, but we also know He is faithful to hear our cries and that our August 13 is coming.

However you came to Christ, the good news is that you came to Him.

Now the story gets interesting. Yes, surgery fixed my shoulder and surgery fixed my ankle, but then the work (i.e., physical therapy) began. Just like we do after surgery, we have to go through therapy to continue our healing after accepting Christ as our Savior. We need therapy, aka being in the Word, fellowshipping with other believers, praying, giving back from what we have been given, worshiping Him even when we aren't in a church building, and doing any of the many other things that lead us to be healed through a relationship with Christ as we walk with Him.

Be blessed!

Your word is a lamp for my feet, a light on my path.

—Psalms 119:105 (NIV)

After I had surgery to fix my ankle, I was back to walking again within five weeks. It was interesting to have something that I had taken for granted become something that required me to think about it. I experienced some pain and discomfort, which I expected, when getting my ankle to work after not using it for seven weeks. And as long as I walked slow, I didn't limp, as my goal was not to develop a limp and have that become a habit. But probably the thing that surprises me the most is how much the first step caused me to think. See, I never know what to expect when I get up to go. Sometimes it is very natural and I just start walking. At other times my ankle feels very unstable and it takes me a few steps to get going. I am sure that in time, the get-up-and-go will be a natural get-up-and-go, especially when I stop thinking about and being overly concerned with what to expect.

Wow, does that sound like how we tend to trust God and His provisions. But it is the first step that is always the hardest. Why? Probably because we don't know what to expect and are concerned that we won't be able to handle it. We are afraid of being on unstable footing, so we cautiously step into having faith in Him and trusting Him. The good news is that at least we take that first step, no matter how unsure we may be. Hopefully as we continue to take those first steps of faith, it will become what we naturally do, just like when one is recovering from something like a broken ankle.

Walk with Him! Be blessed!

Afterword

Now you have read what I have written over the course of three years. I hope that you, whether you read the whole book, some of it, or very little of it, have come across something that was just what you needed to hear about where you were when you happened to read it. More importantly, I hope that you have been encouraged to read, study, and memorize Scripture, the living, breathing Word of God, and to let it speak truth, life, and hope into your life. Hopefully you have been encouraged to spend time in the Word so it will speak to you personally, and hopefully your relationship with the Lord will become more intimate than you could have ever imagined. As 2 Timothy 3:16–17 states, "All scripture is breathed out by God and profitable for teaching, reproof, for correction, and for training in righteousness, that the man of God may be complete, equipped for every good work." So while we walk with Him, we walk in His fullness. Be blessed!

And so now what for me? I don't know, except to say that I know I will be walking with Him.

Made in the USA
San Bernardino, CA
04 September 2016